Aug 27 '86

Charles

Even though you are a "showout" with so many miles over the 9 like normal in running — you anyway!

Blessings

Brooks Faulkner

S0-ARN-911

Forced Termination

NC WESLEYAN COLLEGE LIBRARY
ROCKY MOUNT, NC 27804

North Carolina Wesleyan College Library

Scurry - Drum Collection
Given by:
*Dr. Frank Scurry and
Carolina Evangelical
Divinity School*

Carolina

F263

253.2
fau

543

FORCED TERMINATION

Redemptive Options
for Ministers and Churches

Brooks R. Faulkner

BROADMAN PRESS
Nashville, Tennessee

© Copyright 1986 • Broadman Press
All rights reserved
4254-35
ISBN: 0-8054-5435-7

Dewey Decimal Classification: 253.2
Subject Headings: MINISTERS // CHURCH STAFF
Library of Congress Catalog Card Number: 86-6122
Printed in the United States of America

Unless otherwise noted, all Scripture quotations are taken from the *New American Standard Bible.* Copyright © The Lockman Foundation, 1960, 1962, 1963, 1968, 1971, 1972, 1973, 1975, 1977. Used by permission.

All Scripture quotations marked RSV are taken from the Revised Standard Version of the Bible, copyrighted 1946, 1952, © 1971, 1973.

Library of Congress Cataloging-in-Publication Data

Faulkner, Brooks R.
  Forced termination.

  1. Ex-clergy. 2. Clergy—Office. 3. Church officers.
I. Title.
BV672.5.F38 1986   253'.2   86-6122
ISBN 0-8054-5435-7

Contents

Introduction

He was smiling. The smile was not convincing. His face was red from embarrassment, or anger, or a recently acquired high blood pressure, or all of these.

He began his devotional. The setting was a group of ministers who had recently been dismissed or forced to resign. The place was an associational religious camp near Denton, Texas. The time was early morning and the beginnings of the workshop day.

"Two of the deacons took me to lunch," he began. "I really had no idea what was up. One of the men was and is one of my closest friends, for you see, I still love them.

"One of the men, not my close friend, said, 'Pastor, you know how much we love you. The hardest job I have ever had to do is what we are doing. But, now really, Pastor, don't you think twenty-five years in one church is enough?' "

He paused for an uncomfortably long time. He looked at the group, started to speak, then paused again. He composed himself, then began again.

"I have managed. I am fifty-four years old. But I will survive. My family has stuck with me. Most of my friends have stuck with me. I still feel God has called me to the ministry and I will serve where He places me."

The parting gift of fourteen thousand dollars was hardly

compensation. The hard truth was that he would have to
carry his own retirement program, his insurance program,
his Social Security program, and the livelihood of his family
until he could find another place to serve. Fourteen thousand dollars sounds like a great deal of money. But he
viewed it more as a kind of alimony because his church had
divorced him. They had "rejected". him. They no longer
wanted him. No amount of money can soothe that kind of
pain.

Unfortunately, this happening is not unusual. It is happening among Baptists, Methodists, Presbyterians, Epis-
copalians, Church of the Brethren, Christian churches, and
every denomination in the United States—and even the
world. Some have called it an "epidemic." Perhaps it is no
worse or better than it has been in the past, but it appears
to be worse. Ministers appear to be more willing to talk
about the pain and humiliation of being fired or forced to
resign.

During recent months, I have been in eight states with
workshops designed to give options for consideration to the
ministers who have been fired or forced to resign. In listening to other ministers besides the one whose experience has
just been related, I found that most churches are not so
generous upon termination. In fact, of all the first-person
accounts we heard, this was the most unusual. Perhaps the
twenty-five years was a factor. Perhaps the church truly did
"love" the pastor. It was, nevertheless, unusual.

1. A Natural Disaster?

In 1973 a stunning new idea was developed by Donald P.
Smith in *Clergy in the Cross Fire*. Smith contended that
conflict is a natural part of the order with congregations. "A
number of steps have been suggested by which the minister
can clarify ambiguity and keep conflict to a minimum. But

conflict there will be. The important question is, How is it dealt with?"[1]

The stunning phrase that unsettled our security was, "How is it dealt with?" It is safe to assume that many, perhaps most, ministers who are fired, forced to resign, or simply coerced to resign cannot deal with conflict effectively. That is not a judgment on their morality. It is not necessarily a judgment on their leadership skills. But it is reality. The inability to deal with conflict means that the negotiations have stopped. Persons involved are unwilling or unable to cope with the differences of opinion.

Conflict is natural. When persons care about each other, conflict will occur. It happens in families. It happens among friends. It happens in politics. It also happens in churches.

People in churches have a tendency to be religious. Being religious may mean becoming critical of those who are not the same kind of religious we are. For example, Matthew 15:1-4 reads: "Then some Pharisees and scribes came to Jesus from Jerusalem, saying, 'Why do Your disciples transgress the tradition of the elders? For they do not wash their hands when they eat bread.' And He answered and said to them, 'And why do you yourselves transgress the commandment of God for the sake of your tradition? For God said, 'Honor your father and mother,' and, 'He who speaks evil of Father or mother, let him be put to death.'"

Matthew 12:1-4 reads: "At that time Jesus went on the Sabbath through the grainfields, and His disciples became hungry and began to pick the heads of grain and eat. But when the Pharisees saw it, they said to Him, 'Behold, your disciples do what is not lawful to do on a Sabbath.' But He said to them, 'Have you not read what David did, when he became hungry, he and his companions; how he entered the house of God, and they ate the consecrated bread, which was not lawful for him to eat, nor for those with him, but for the priests alone?'"

It is also natural for ministers to cause conflict with churches—and each other. It is far too easy to call churches the heavies in a forced termination episode and forget the ministers who have created the conflict for themselves. Paul wrote, "But when Cephas came to Antioch, I opposed him to his face, because he stood condemned. For prior to the coming of certain men from James, he used to eat with the Gentiles; but when they came, he began to withdraw and hold himself aloof, fearing the party of the circumcision. And the rest of the Jews joined him in hypocrisy, with the result that even Barnabas was carried away by their hypocrisy" (Gal. 2:11-13). *Hypocrisy* was and is a volatile word. When one minister calls another minister a hypocrite, it is predictable that there will be some form of conflict.

Very few who attend associational meetings, state convention meetings, or conventions on a national level of any denomination doubt that conflict is natural. Religious persons, even Christian religious persons, are going to have conflict. It is natural because we are human. All of us. Ministers are also human. We do not always like it or admit it, but we are. It is sometimes disappointing for laypersons to accept this, much less believe it. That may be all the more infuriating to them. They find out their minister is human, and their disappointment cannot be hidden when a critical issue emerges where it can be shown.

2. Misunderstanding: The Villain

One church member explained his dilemma: "Our church has never understood ministers. They come in like a house afire. They witness. They preach stimulating sermons. They work hard at getting along with persons. Then something happens. They become bored, or disenchanted, or both. What makes them that way? We have never understood. The result is that our church changes ministers every two or three years. The last eight or ten ministers have left under duress. They leave or we ask them to leave. The bottom line is that we do not understand ministers."

I wondered as this young deacon was explaining this misunderstanding of ministers what the last eight or ten ministers might say about this church of which he was a member. Would they feel they did not understand the church in the same way that the church did not understand them?

Robert Bolton feels this problem of misunderstanding is an everywhere problem, not just a church problem. "Proximity without intimacy is inevitably destructive."[2] He feels that when people exist together and do not develop love for each other, then the caring will eventually stop. When the caring stops, something happens to the ability to get along with each other. When persons do not get along, they misunderstand one another.

One reason why ministers are misunderstood is that they get a minimum of feedback. Few church members are willing to give feedback to the minister. Those who do mostly give negative feedback. Those who emulate the minister give feedback which is hardly objective. It is one-sided. It gives him the adulation and adoration that he may need but may not help him to see things in perspective. Few members know how to give straight and honest feedback which includes both positive and negative feedback.

When a minister receives a minimum of feedback from church members who feel a maximum need to give feedback, it is hardly surprising that the eruption is just a matter of "when." Ministers need more avenues for feedback. Church members need to be more bold and courageous in giving feedback. It will help them care more for the minister. It will help the minister to get a feel of the pulse of the attitudes and feelings of the church members.

In Black Mountain, North Carolina a group of ministers who had been forced to resign was listening to a thirty-five-year-old minister tell of the eruptive episode in his church. It had happened two months earlier. The chairman of deacons had a son who was arrested for drug possession. The whole community was concerned. The relationship between the pastor and the chairman of deacons had not been satisfactory to the pastor, and he felt this would be one way to improve the relationship. He decided to take the initiative. He called the chairman of deacons to make an appointment.

Upon arrival, he was treated coolly. "I've come to see if I could be of some assistance," he said.

"What do you mean, assistance?" asked the chairman of deacons. "You're delighted to see me in this fix. You've been waiting to get something on me. How dare you come to my house at a time like this with me in a situation like this? You can leave my house. I don't want you back until I give you an invitation."

The minister said he felt devastated. He said he did not understand then. He still does not understand. But two weeks later the minister was brought before the deacons on what the minister described as "trumped-up" charges. He did not elaborate. He was asked to resign. All nineteen deacons voted to ask him.

Later in the week, the minister shared with the other participants that this was the third church that had asked him to resign. To have been the recipient of that much anger in that many different situations, he was not being understood either. Some misunderstanding must have developed long before the tender feelings of the deacon were exposed. It takes at least two to create misunderstanding.

3. Someone May Get Burned

Although very few give credit to Harry S. Truman for its originality, he was famous for the adage, "If you can't stand the heat, get out of the kitchen." The meaning seems clear.

If you can't take conflict, don't get near it. And there will be conflict in the kitchen (in this case, a church).

In politics, the adage may be applicable. However, the spiritual symmetry of the church members is not at stake in politics. A politician can afford to be abrasive at times. He can be aggressive with policy which he has the authority to deal with on his own. A minister does not view conflict in the same manner. Many ministers view their work as highly dependent upon being well liked and well accepted. If they were to become Trumanistic, they feel they would surely get burned.

Alienation is a feared possibility. When the heat gets hot in the kitchen, alienation becomes more than a possibility. It is more a probability. Someone will be alienated in a church when the heat of conflict gets out of hand. It takes a steady hand and/or hands to keep conflict in a continuum of redemption.

Larry L. McSwain and William C. Treadwell, Jr., in their book *Conflict Ministry in the Church,* feel the reason for this kind of unmanageable heat is stress or anxiety on one or both parts. "Often one or the other of the two parties is experiencing unusual stress or anxiety and becomes unable to control the flow of emotions which hurt and alienate people."[3]

Church conflict becomes even more personal, feel McSwain and Treadwell, because the stresses "encountered by ministry leaders from within a church setting are focused upon those closest to them, families, and fellow workers, even though the roots of stress are elsewhere."[4] The result is that the heat in the kitchen of church conflict nearly always burns or alienates someone. The persons have been previously so close that it is like a divorce. A marriage that reaches an impasse rarely ends without someone getting burned. A church is a family. The roots of the stress may be somewhere else, but the minister or the deacon or a family member between these persons who work closely together may become the focus of the heat.

4. Oversupply?

Some have suggested that the reason some churches have become so independent in choosing and keeping a minister is because of the oversupply of ministers. A disturbing research project and resulting book suggesting this possibility was completed in 1980 by Jackson W. Carroll and Robert L. Wilson. *Too Many Pastors?* suggests that in the Southern Baptist Convention alone, the ratio of clergy to churches increased from 0.8 to 1.6 from 1950 to 1977 and the projections for the year 2000 are 2.6.[5] That means that from 1950 to 2000, the increase of clergy to churches will have been 1.8. There will be almost three ministers for each church. Of course the projections are relative, and the anticipation of beginning new churches and missions is highly incalculable; but the projections nevertheless are rather frightening.

To bring it closer to home, one might ask the chairman of a pastor selection committee or minister selection committee how many resumés they have received. I was interim pastor of a small church in Tennessee. The chairman of the pastor selection committee received forty-four resumés. Some of the resumés were from friends and supporters of others. Some were from the possible candidates themselves.

One must consider the fact that many are unhappy and want to move. Some ministers simply want to move for whatever purpose. But there appear to be more than enough candidates for every church ministry position.

And churches are aware. Church members know that there are numerous resumés sent and recommended when their church is without a pastor or another staff member. In a deacon's conference in Missouri, one bright young deacon shared that he had just completed his role as chairman of a pastor selection committee. He suggested that his church could have called any number of a dozen persons. He said his church received over two hundred resumés. In his words, they could have had "the pick of the litter."

The reasons for possible oversupply and the resulting psychology of reaction on church members are far from simple. Carroll and Wilson contend: "By the early 1970s economic and other pressures brought cutbacks in nonparish ministry positions, which reduced demand and also increased the supply of active clergy seeking available positions. Finally, rising costs of goods and services, and losses of membership combined to slow, if not reverse, the trend toward full-time clergy for small congregations and additional staff for large congregations. The result is the current oversupply of clergy or at least an increasingly tight job market."[6]

Although the situation may not be as simple as the findings of Carroll and Wilson suggest, the reality of the mentality of oversupply is evident in how church members respond to calling a minister. The reasons may not be clear in the mind of the chairman of the minister selection committee. The reality is accepted in the mind of the chairman of the minister selection committee: "Our church can have the pick of the litter."

Notes

1. Donald P. Smith, *Clergy in the Cross Fire* (Philadelphia: Westminster Press, 1973), p. 95.

2. Robert Bolton, *People Skills* (Englewood Cliffs: Prentice-Hall, 1979), p. 6.

3. Larry L. McSwain and William C. Treadwell, Jr., *Conflict Ministry in the Church* (Nashville: Broadman Press, 1981), p. 102.

4. Ibid., p. 107.

5. Jackson W. Carroll and Robert L. Wilson, *Too Many Pastors?* (New York: Pilgrim Press, 1977), p. 36.

6. Ibid., pp. 61-62.

1
Why Ministers Become Expendable

Long before ministers are terminated, either voluntarily or involuntarily, they become expendable in the minds of the legitimizers or power brokers in the churches. In other words, these legitimizers begin to feel that the church could get along without them. They may feel the church would be *better off* without them. How does a minister get to this place in the minds of these church members? Why does he permit himself or herself to become expendable?

No simple answer exists. However, I have made judgments based on some feedback from some ministers and church members who have been involved in forced termination workshops.

1. Rigidity

One reason ministers become expendable is rigidity. Rigidity is a problem for either (or both) the minister and the church. If the church is rigid in the expectations of the minister, an impasse is inevitable. If the minister is rigid in the expectations of the church, an impasse is inevitable. Rigidity will alienate.

Rigidity can be summarized in one way as the belief that "I am right and you are wrong; I will act accordingly." If I feel that I am right and you are wrong, I will be blinded in what I hear from you. In fact, I may not hear you at all. If, then, I decide not to hear you, I will believe that what you say is not worth hearing. The result of that complicated rigidity is that the person trying to respond to me will feel that I think him or her of no worth. It is quite natural, then, that the rigidity will lead to alienation.

Rigidity occurs when there is no communication. I can talk to you without really communicating with you. If I become rigid, no amount of talk from you will convince me that I am wrong. It follows that that kind of talk is not positive communication. Positive communication can only occur when both hear and both respond as if the other person has worth.

Carl Rogers, from whom many ministers learned listening technique in communication/counseling, believes the major barrier to interpersonal communication lies in our very natural tendency to judge—to approve or disapprove of the statements of the other person.[1] A minister, by his very vocation, judges what is good and what is bad. He mirrors the biblical concept of sin to others, and that is judgment. The sensitive person who observes the minister's judicial role is tempted to feel the drama of the judgment in what otherwise may be an innocent and innocuous activity. Sensitive persons are likely to see even the tenderest minister as rigid and judicial simply because of what they have grown accustomed to seeing.

One church member said of his pastor, "You *cannot* talk to him." The church member virtually yelled the words *cannot*. "I have tried," he said. "We were getting a lot of flak about how long he was preaching. When 12:00 PM rolls around, our people begin to get restless. He seemed to defy the restlessness. He reacted to it with such strong feelings that from 12:00 PM until he wrapped it up, you could predict that we were going to get the dickens. He preached more and more negatively after 12:00. The message we

heard from him (at least the under-the-table message) was
'You sit there and be quiet. I am a man of God and when you
question me you question God.' He may not have meant it
that way, but that is the way our people perceived it.

"Well, I am not known for being passive. So I was kind of
unofficially appointed to see if I could talk to him. I had been
able to talk to our two previous pastors as a brother, so I
thought I would give it a shot.

"You just wouldn't believe how nice he was. He smiled
graciously at me when I told him I thought a lot of people
viewed his preaching past 12:00 as a way of telling us not
to question God. He said he would give it some thought. But
you guessed it. The next Sunday he went until almost 12:40,
and the negative outlook was even more evident than
before. It was like he was two different persons. *Rigid* is a
nice word for how he acted. Perhaps stubborn or hardhead-
ed would be more accurate."

Obviously, there was more to this story. The church member was giving only one view. I did not hear the pastor's
point of view. I was not surprised when he said, "We finally
had to let him go."

When I reflected on the story this church member told of
his terminated pastor, the word *terminated* seemed to fit.
From the words "We finally had to let him go," I felt as
much rigidity as he said the pastor had. Rigidity is a two-
edged sword.

2. Tenure: "He's Been Here Too Long!"

The findings of a research project conducted by the Alban
Institute in 1980 were published in a booklet, "Should the
Pastor be Fired?" *How to Deal Constructively with Clergy-
Lay Conflict.* The first item listed under "What Criteria Can
be Brought to Bear to Make a Judgment for Termination?"
was "Length of Tenure."[2]

Some churches have a mind-set about a minister's length

of tenure. Some feel three years is long enough. Others feel five years is long enough. Only the omniscient Father knows where these designated lengths of time come from. But they are there.

I was involved in a training experience one Sunday night as a layman. It was awkward because I had been a minister in churches for most of my adult life. I had concluded an interim pastorate and was determined to become "just another church member." Bob was chairman of deacons and one of those members who had become the heart of the church. He was in the training group with me. Bob was a former Methodist who had joined this Baptist church where I now belonged. The church was without a pastor at the time, and we were studying the pastor's role in a church.

When we got to the area of the pastor's responsibility for motivating persons, Bob became agitated. "One reason pastors cannot motivate people is that they stay too long."

"How long is too long?" I asked Bob.

"Five years is maximum."

I asked where the number five came from. He suggested that in the Methodist church you could predict that the pastor would be moved in about five years (or even less) unless there were very unusual circumstances. Since most of my vocational time is spent in helping ministers wrestle with their stability in ministry, I was angry. I overreacted. I strongly urged him to take another look at what he was saying because I felt a minister should become a permanent part of the church he serves. He is not a temporary visitor, but a permanent shepherd. Unless church members can gain that perspective, a pastor will always be viewed as a "passing-through" minister. He is temporary.

One church member suggested when we called a minister, "Well, if we don't like him, maybe the next one will be better. I was here before he came, and I will be here when he is gone." This is evidence of her feelings of the pastor's being temporary.

Our minister has now been in our church for eight years. Each of the last three years has been a victory. These are silent, subtle, and enigmatic victories, but they are dramatic to me. Bob has become one of the strongest supporters of our minister. I would like to think the reason was a part of what I said that night some eight and one-half years ago. I am not that naive. He was playing an old Methodist tape. It could just have easily been a Baptist tape, or Episcopalian, ad infinitum. Somewhere, sometime, someone has taught many church members that a minister's effectiveness is over after three to five years. Better understanding helped Bob become more tolerant and less rigid.

The dangers are there. After eighteen to twenty-six months, a minister who deals with the process of leadership will go through a critical period. Research has proven that the first real test of his or her leadership comes during this period. But the aggressive minister who is growing in the job and his or her life will read the process and correct and adjust. The rigid minister will not. The minister who feels he or she has already been there long enough will not.

Sam Granade, until his retirement in 1984 as Church Minister Relations Director in Alabama, worked with ministers who were forced to resign for the last twelve years of his ministry. Before that, he was pastor of one church in Alabama for twenty-two years. In July 1983 the two of us conducted a workshop for ministers and their wives who had suffered forced resignation. In discussing the subject of tenure, Sam made the observation that he did not become pastor of the church until after five years. He said he could not recall the exact incident. But there were several tests to his leadership that seemed to reach solution after about five years. Until that time, he said, he was their preacher.

He compared the situation to a wife who is testing her

husband. In a sense, she is giving off a lot of negative signals to see if the husband will run. It is not that the wife does not love the husband. Far from it. The wife wants to know if the husband is going to be there when she needs him the most. So, in a temporary fit of neurosis, the wife lashes out at the husband. If he really loves her, he will stay. Sam stayed. The love relationship with his church grew stronger and stronger. The result: twenty-two years and a growing relationship.

Some of the findings of the research team of the Alban Institute included reasons why some ministers have long-term relationships with churches. The congregations

"Are able to care for their own members as well as others.

"Accept clergy as human beings, and allow room for them to fail.

"Have the ability to work through issues. When trouble occurs, a problem-solving attitude is adopted, rather than a blaming attitude."[3]

Additionally, the ministers themselves resist the temptation to draw to themselves people who are similar. Annual projects are never taken for granted. The ministerial leadership does not take for granted that the lay leadership will do what they want. Decisions are always referred for consultation and action.[4]

"Too long" is a relative term. Too long is rarely a reason for forcing the termination of one of God's servants who is doing what God wants him or her to do.

3. Subterranean Pastors

Some ministers are called. Some have an office of minister. But some who are not called and who do not have an office of minister, in reality, pastor a church. Almost all persons with whom I have worked in the area of pastoral leadership agree: Every church has more than one pastor or minister.

The view from an insecure minister would be that these are persons who would usurp the authority of the pastor. These ministers feel they must "stand their ground" or they will be sucked up into oblivion from leadership effectiveness. But this view is not always accurate.

"Subterranean" pastors care for the church. They are also concerned about their own spiritual leadership. These subterranean pastors may be men or women. They may be rich or poor. They may be active or quasi-active. But in their own minds, and in the minds of many church members, the real spiritual leader of the church emerges during critical and dramatic periods of the church. The real spiritual leader is usually him- or herself and not the pastor.

I have a theory about subterranean pastors. I suspect there are two, not one. I suspect one of the subterranean pastors is angry because he or she is not the pastor. Of course, the subterranean pastor may not know consciously what he or she is angry about. The anger often surfaces during business meetings. It surfaces during issues that are critical to the spiritual health of the church. The office of the pastor, and not necessarily the pastor as a person, becomes a serious threat to this subterranean pastor. The pastor may become the enemy. In the minds of some church members the pastor can do no wrong; but in the mind of this subterranean pastor, the pastor can do no right. The sparks begin to fly when the subterranean pastor fixes himself or herself in a win-lose position. Sometimes he or she wins. The pastor is forced to resign.

There is another subterranean pastor. This pastor is much more positive in behavior. He prays for the pastor. He talks of the pastor's welfare. Frequently, he is responsible for increases in the pastor's salary. He supports the hard-to-get-to-support activities. He visits and witnesses for Christ. He is quick to accept menial tasks and positions. He uses the spiritual language of the Bible as well as, or perhaps better than, the pastor himself. This person is looked to when the issue being considered in the church is unclear. He or she is expected to give clarity, and usually this person does so with a cool head. He cares for the church.

I have a moral to this theory of two subterranean pastors. "Never do battle with the spiritual subterranean pastor." It is a no-win situation. The best approach is to work with this person, who can be a stellar part of the ministry. Most of them have no desire to usurp the pastor's authority. Most are satisfied when the pastor is seen as effective and loved. There is no need to be jealous of him or her. The danger comes when the pastor positions himself against this person, perhaps feeling threatened.

The best biblical example of this second type of subterranean pastor is Barnabas. Young Saul came back to Jerusalem from Damascus, and all the disciples were suspicious and/or afraid of him. Barnabas vouched for him. He urged the disciples to believe that Saul was sincere in the change. The church in Jerusalem sent Barnabas to investigate the church at Antioch, engaged in a racial issue in which cool heads were needed. The fact that they sent Barnabas showed their confidence and esteem (Acts 11:19-26).

Later Paul and Barnabas parted ways, partly because of a disagreement over Mark. But years later, when Paul wrote to the church at Corinth, he spoke kindly of Barnabas. "Or do only Barnabas and I not have a right to refrain from working?" (1 Cor. 9:6). It was out of context for the subject of liberty, but Paul spoke of him as an inseparable colleague, which Barnabas was. The name Barnabas literally means "son of consolation."[5] In every church I have been in there was a Barnabas, a "son of consolation." A subterranean pastor will help the ministry of the pastor if the pastor is not threatened by his or her power and spiritual strength.

One of the parenthetical dilemmas for the minister is

especially interesting. It should be remembered that the first subterranean pastor is frequently frightened of the second subterranean pastor. The first, the nonspiritual type, will go to great lengths to gather allies for his or her cause. If the first type can get the spiritual type on his or her side against the pastor, all the better. But if this is impossible, it has been my experience that the first type will then try to get the pastor to become an ally against the second type. The first subterranean pastor seems to relish the idea of conflict and disturbance.

The response might be, to be effective as a minister one must become a wizard at human relationships. One must know what is happening before it happens. I really believe that. A minister must be effective at understanding complex human relationships. He or she must be effective at predicting what might be, based on what is now going on in the church. This is important, not only for the sake of keeping the stability of the job, but for ministering effectively.

4. Deaconphobia

Deaconphobia is the "fear of deacons." One reason ministers become expendable is their fear of deacons. By and large, the situation is not that simple. But the reality is there. Many pastors simply have an innate fear of deacons.

Listen carefully to a Monday morning gathering of a group of ministers who have just exhaled from an out-of-breath Sunday. You will hear one, two, or more allusions to the deacons who made life miserable on the day before.

No one knows why exactly. Deacons are usually fair people. Most are kind, considerate, and humble. They have been elected by their peers. Therefore, they have earned respect. Although biblically, the pattern for deacons has meant "service" in the spiritual sense of the word, many deacons have taken their office and felt it to mean administration. These deacons administer the work of the church.

In the truest sense of the word, to some deacons, they are responsible for "supervising" the work of the minister.

Whatever the reason, many ministers have grown to treat deacons with a kind of arms-length relationship. That caution has led to fear for many.

This relationship is reciprocal. Treat someone with fear, and he returns the favor. Many deacons feel the minister must be watched. They fear the minister in much the same way that the minister fears the deacons.

Unless the gap can be bridged, deacons will grow to feel they can get along without the minister. If he is fearful, he is in doubt about his ability. If *he* is in doubt about his ability, then why shouldn't *they* be in doubt about his ability? The result of this form of paranoia is deaconphobia. Deaconphobia will lead to the feeling that the minister is expendable.

5. Loss of Respect or Trust

Churches have traditions. The opening chorus in the musical *Fiddler on the Roof* is "Tradition." It sets the stage for the entire musical. The courtship and marriage of the daughters must follow the traditions. Things should be done a certain way. Tradition is revered. Churches become steeped in tradition. Things should be done a certain way.

Ministers are models for good behavior. If a minister is volatile and is known to explode on occasion, some churches become intolerant. Some become unforgiving. Traditionally, a minister is kind and considerate even in the face of strong adversity. If a minister breaks that tradition, he loses respect. Often, it takes a long period of reconstruction to rebuild.

It can become even more unsettling. If a church has a tradition of beginning a worship service at 11:00 AM on Sunday morning, and an innovative minister of youth suggests a change to 9:00 AM to precede the Bible teaching

NC WESLEYAN COLLEGE LIBRARY
ROCKY MOUNT, NC 27804

period, some may lose respect. "What's she trying to do? Why is she so radical? This is 'our' church. How does she dare to come in here and upset things!"

It makes little difference that the change was for the purpose of reaching more people. The church was located on a southern beach, and many of the younger people and younger couples were leaving after the Bible teaching period to go to the beach. The minister of youth suggested to the pastor that they try the earlier service, and the pastor went along. The personnel committee met in haste. The minister of youth was called on the carpet. So was the pastor. After all, he recommended the minister of youth.

"Why?" the minister of youth was asked.

She explained.

"Why didn't you go through the proper channels?" she was asked.

She didn't think they would mind if they could reach more people, she responded.

They compromised. They began both worship services. Eventually, this church changed to the earlier service altogether. But the minister of youth, in relating this story, felt she was never trusted after this event. She left the church just a few months later. She felt she left just in time to keep herself from being fired.

Of course, loss of respect or trust will come following immoral behavior. Both the minister and the church should expect that. What the minister may not expect is what peculiar "traditions" must be revered. For example, in some churches, a pulpit robe is acceptable. Maybe it is required. In other churches, it would be amusing. If the minister acts with insensitivity to either tradition, he is flirting with disaster in his leadership respectability.

In some churches, informality is expected. If there is more than one minister, traditionally, all may speak at several different periods in the worship experience. This may, in the mind of the congregation, lend "warmth." In other churches, however, to speak informally would be totally unacceptable behavior. The minister can expect to be called on the carpet. He can anticipate losing respect and trust because he has violated one of the traditions of the church.

In summary of gaining or losing respect and trust, if the minister respects the traditions, respect will follow. If the minister does not respect the traditions, he or she will find it hard to win respect and trust from the laypersons.

We may be tempted to blast the "sacred cows" of tradition that the eighth-century prophets blasted. Amos, Hosea, Micah, and Isaiah showed a great deal of disdain for the traditions which mocked God. But it is important to remember that most of us do not live in a world like the one the eighth-century prophets lived in. It is not as easy for us to determine the "sacred cows" as it was for the prophets. They were personally acquainted with the Baalites and their prophets. Traditions in churches in America are much more subtle. Indeed, some of the traditions are worth keeping. We would do well to have respect for the character of the membership which has developed traditions. Trust the church members who have guarded them. Some may need changing. Some may be "sacred cows." But treating them gently means you have respect for the persons who have developed the traditions. These church members will reciprocate by respecting and trusting the minister.

6. Incompetence

One additional reason why ministers become expendable is incompetence. Most ministers would enjoy the feeling that the call of God makes them competent. It does not. The call into ministry is a beginning. The price for preparation must be paid.

When I was called into the ministry, I felt the phrase "called to preach" was adequate to describe my vocational direction. I did not know about the rigors of administration, pastoral care, long-term shepherding, interpersonal relationships, grief ministry, or motivation. I did not know that a part of my work would be to effectively supervise a church staff. I was simply "called to preach."

But most churches want a pastor, not simply a preacher. Most churches want a minister of education who is versatile in leadership skills. Most churches want a minister of music who is adept at witnessing as well as being a musician. In other words, churches want much more than they bargain for in calling a staff member. They expect it. They are entitled.

Churches have a right to expect competence. They do not have a right to expect more than the minister can produce. They do have a right to expect the minister to continue to grow in skills.

Competence for a minister can be divided into two parts: personal skills and interpersonal skills.

A. Personal Skills

The minister should be skilled at *communication*. He or she should be able to get through to persons and permit persons to get through to them. Without the skill of communication, the minister can "hang it up," as they say. Workshops, seminars, conferences, and reading materials are available to help the minister update skills in communication.

The minister should be skilled at *motivation*. Motivation is the ability to unleash the potential of others. To motivate means to create the "want to."

The minister should be skilled at *delegation*. The minister should be able to share ministry. The minister should be able to give his or her job away.

A minister should be able to *plan and evaluate*. He or she

should be able to look ahead and see what should and needs to be done.

The minister should be skilled at *time management*. Work hours for the minister are usually unlike the work hours of those ministered to. But managing time well is a part of modeling good personal skills. If the minister is unpredictable to the point of negligence, disapproval will come. Effective time management involves making a serious effort to allot time for the essentials in ministry. Office hours which are predictable help responsible church members know that they have a responsible minister.

In spite of the complaints of some ministers that their time is never their own, it has been my experience that most church members are understanding. If the minister will take the time to communicate to responsible persons how they spend their time, most church members appreciate the fact that they trust them enough to share. For example, the busiest day of the week for the minister is Sunday. Sunday is filled with worship experiences, preparation for worship experiences, committee meetings, impromptu emergencies from concerned church members, and the general casual shepherding which is a part of the life of any minister. In no way can it be considered as a day of rest.

But the minister should take a day of rest. Additionally, the minister should communicate what day the day of rest will be. This day of rest should be taken in addition to the "day off" to which every minister is entitled. Managing time will help the minister grow in personal skills. Managing time well shows church members that the minister feels personal skills should continue to be developed and never taken for granted.

If the minister supervises a staff, or if the staff is being supervised, the personal skill required is giving and taking *supervision*. This skill requires a healthy outlook on authority. It requires a responsible response to the fact that all of us who give guidance need guidance for ourselves. The development of supervision skills is a grossly neglected area for us religious folk.

B. Interpersonal Skills

In 1979 Ronald Forgus and Bernard H. Shulman developed a college and university textbook on the understanding of interpersonal behavior. The book, *Personality: A Cognitive View*, suggests that one reason why social relationships are difficult for persons is distorted goals. Some of the distorted goals are:

"To be without flaw"

"To be more impressive than anyone else"

"To be the center of attention"

"To be always loved"

"To never submit"

"To avoid unpleasantness"

"To master everything."[6]

If we look carefully, we may discover why some ministers find interpersonal relationships so difficult. "To be without flaw" means we present ourselves to others in a manner that shows no weaknesses. Most church members suspect we are human, but nourish their myth that the minister is perfect if we do not refute it. Is there anything any more infuriating than to find a flaw in one who says he or she has none?

"To be more impressive than anyone else" means someone must be put down.

"To be the center of attention" means church members may go unnoticed; and when unnoticed, some feel unworthy.

"To be always loved" is the hope of an immature and perhaps neurotic person. Only therapists find this person interesting.

"To never submit" invites combat. To the combative and

angry church member, this is an invitation to emotional war.

"To avoid unpleasantness" may indicate lack of strength. Few church members want to be around a Pollyanna. An optimistic person is one thing; an abdicating leader is quite another.

"To master everything" is the dream of a child. In professional basketball, a term has been developed called "role player." A "role player" is one who knows his abilities and his limitations and can act them out without feeling humiliation. A minister who has mastered his knowledge of abilities and limitations is far more interpersonally acceptable than one who feels he must "master everything." The "role player" in basketball goes in for three or four minutes to guard the person who is having a hot streak. His role is to shut the other team down by playing tough sticky defense. When the opponent has cooled off, the role player comes out of the game.

The minister who is content to live with his abilities and limitations knows that there are some businessmen in the church who can deal with the bids on a vacant lot the church wishes to purchase better than he can. It is not demeaning to him to permit someone who is more competent to be the role player. Nor is it demeaning for him to be a role player for the church.

Maslow characterized the person who is able to make interpersonal relationships a reality as "self-actualized." The following traits make up a partial list of characteristics necessary for "self-actualized" persons in effective interpersonal relationships.

"acceptance of self, others, and nature"
"spontaneity and ingenuousness"
"a capacity for deep interpersonal relationships"
"an authentic sense of human values"
"a sense of humor"

Forced Termination

"creative thinking"
"a strong sense of belonging."[7]
This does not mean that persons who are "self-actualized" will not have enemies. On the contrary, it means that the person with these traits will be able to cope with enemies. The minister with interpersonal skills similar to those on the Maslow list will more likely be viewed as competent than the person who does not have these skills.

In this chapter, we have dealt with "Why Ministers Become Expendable." In the next chapter, we will deal with "Why Churches Become Dissatisfied with Ministers." Often, these two segments have overlapping similarities. They are, however, distinctly different in many ways.

Notes

1. Carl Rogers, *On Becoming a Person* (Boston: Houghton-Mifflin, 1961), p. 330.
2. "Should the Pastor Be Fired?" *How to Deal Constructively with Clergy-Laity Conflict* (Washington, D.C.: The Alban Institute, Inc., 1980), p. 7.
3. Ibid., p. 8.
4. Ibid.
5. *Master Study Bible* (Nashville: Holman Bible Publishers, 1981), p. 1670.
6. Ronald Forgus and Bernard H. Shulman, *Personality: A Cognitive View* (Englewood Cliffs: Prentice-Hall, 1979), p. 107.
7. Ibid., p. 227.

2

Why Churches Become Dissatisfied with Ministers

Why do churches become dissatisfied with ministers? If ministers could find a satisfactory answer to that question, they could save themselves a great deal of grief. If churches could find a satisfactory answer to that question, they could be much more selective in choosing their ministers. In turn, they could save themselves a great deal of grief.

There are some indications. These indications of dissatisfaction are not always clear. But some can be identified.

1. Stress Within the Congregation

In 1980 Speed Leas of the Alban Institute of Washington, D.C. did a study of involuntary terminations of ministers with three denominations: Episcopal, United Churches of Christ, and some Presbyterian churches. One of the major issues, perhaps *the* major issue of congregations who terminate ministers, is "Factions in the congregation. Often these difficulties go back many years, sometimes to a merger, to family feuds, an old decision about whether or not to build a building, or a theological difference."[1]

If this is true in most denominations, and not just the three denominations studied, this would jeopardize the future of the minister even before he begins his ministry. He or she would be caught in the middle through no fault of

33

their own. Of the churches studied, "40% of the Episcopal churches, 34% of the United Churches of Christ, and 45% of the Presbyterian churches had existing conflict or problems in the congregation before the terminated pastor started his or her job. This suggests that congregations which terminate pastors do have a higher incidence of conflict than congregations where terminations have not taken place."2

The similarity is that of a police officer trying to break up a family conflict or squabble. Often, statistics have proven, it is the police officer who becomes the recipient of the wrath of the husband and wife. They both turn on the police officer, the innocent party, because this is an infringement on their privacy.

The analogy is understandable. The minister infringes upon the privacy of the family having a family squabble. He has not yet become a member of the family. Their wrath is then vented upon the new invader.

2. Neighboring Churches Are Growing

We live in a competitive society. Business is competitive. Educational accomplishments are competitive. Sports are competitive. It is difficult for the church not to join the mood. When a church becomes competitive, comparisons are made. If other churches are growing, then something must be wrong with us if we are not growing.

3. Spiritually Stagnant

Another reason why churches become restless with ministers is that they feel they have become spiritually stagnant. "He just doesn't feed us anymore" is a statement often heard from church members who are looking for something inspiring from the minister during worship experiences.

If the zest is gone in our spiritual lives, then we must look to where we feel the emptiness is. Often the emptiness can be pinpointed to the Sunday services. If the Sunday services are not living up to our expectations, there must be a reason. That reason is often the minister.

4. If You Don't Win Games, You Fire the Coach

It's an American tradition. If you don't win games, you fire the coach. Our church is not growing like other churches. We feel the spiritual stagnation. Our minister can find another church just as a coach can find another team. We watch the American tradition and get caught up in that mentality.

Winning games can be compared to reaching more people. Or building larger buildings. Or raising larger budgets. Or building larger staffs. Comparisons are made to neighboring churches which are growing; why aren't we? It is easier to fire the coach than to turn the team around from within. The energy necessary for turning a church around from within is an enormous amount. This means that laypersons will have to expend time as well as energy. It means laypersons will become responsible. It is easier to get a new coach and begin from without.

5. He Can't Get Along with "Key" People

If you talk to ten church members they may give ten different responses to the question of who the "key" people in the church are. But one deacon, in describing the difficulties of the minister who was just terminated, said, "He just could not get along with the key people in the church."

From the church's point of view, it is essential for the minister to get along with these key people. There are some church members who make strong demands for attention. Other church members need to be cultivated with warmth and affection. Others would like to be consulted about their opinion on critical issues. Still others are trusted by large groups of persons within the church, and it becomes expedient for the minister to confide in these persons. But it is no easy task to decipher who the key people are in any church. But one fact remains: the minister's stability will rest on the ability to find these key people and work through them—or around them.

One minister in Alabama who attended a Forced Resignation Workshop told a story of a "key" person who sounded much like someone out of the old West. Except for the pain in his eyes and the concern in his voice, we might have considered the story completely apocryphal. A young lady, about twenty-one years of age, approached the new minister one Wednesday evening just before the monthly business meeting. She said, "You haven't been by to see me yet. After you have consulted with some of the church members you will learn that very few major decisions are made in this church without consulting me first. You didn't consult with me before bringing up this matter of an electric typewriter which you think the church office needs. I would not suggest you bother with that tonight."

The minister said it sounded as if she had some problems, but he decided to go ahead with the business meeting agenda as planned. When the proposal for the typewriter was presented, she stood and spoke against it quite eloquently, he thought. She then made a motion that they table the proposal. The church voted against it. The main motion was then passed. She got up out of the business meeting and left.

In about ten minutes she returned, with her husband behind her. The minister said he looked every bit of twelve feet tall. She interrupted the business meeting and said, "Ever since I was fifteen, the pastors here have consulted with me. You are the first minister to insult me in front of my friends. You should have listened to me."

With that, the husband lifted a pistol and aimed it at the minister. By this time the deacons had surrounded the minister, while one deacon began reasoning with the young couple. Another deacon joined the caucus. After several emotional appeals, the young couple was escorted out of the church. The minister did not press charges.

From that night on, late-night phone calls and open threats were a daily occurrence. The young woman had lots of family members in the community. The minister's tires were slit on more than one occasion. After six months of harassment, the minister's wife had to be hospitalized from stress. The minister resigned without having another church.

Fortunately, not many churches have this kind of problem with "key" people; but several ministers we talked to felt the story was credible because of the similarities to their own situation.

From a different point of view, when some church members talk about "key" people, they are speaking of the subterranean pastors mentioned earlier or about their own allies.

One charge against a minister of education who was being considered for forced termination was that he took pride in "not playing politics." "It is a matter of pride for him," the chairman of the Personnel Committee said. "He wants the church to know that he is his own man." His shrug indicated his frustration. "We all knew he was his own man until he started having to prove it."

It is an opinion. But what many church members consider an inability to get along with key people is in reality (to them, at least) an unwillingness to work with authority.

6. His Manner and Presence Are Offensive

Most churches take great pride in their ministers. They want them to be persons who make a pleasant and impressive presence. Personally, I feel they have a right to that expectation. They need not be handsome or physically attractive. But church members expect cleanliness and good hygiene.

In March 1983, after the first Forced Resignation Workshop we conducted in Missouri, our state papers carried a number of articles about the workshop. Most of the letters were from ministers and their families. But some of the letters were from church members who were concerned that the press releases were presenting a one-sided picture. One such letter from "A member of a congregation that is praying for the pastor to leave," wrote:

"I would like to comment on the article . . . about firing the pastor. Many articles similar to yours have been printed recently and they all place the blame on the congregation.

"Our pastor has a beautiful home to live in, all utilities paid, a car expense, retirement, and hospital insurance all paid by the congregation.

"Now for the pastor. His sermons are dull to the point of boring. His hygiene is the worst I have ever seen; dirty hair with dandruff so bad it shows through the hair, food in his teeth, bad breath, etc. He gets up about 9:00 (nine o'clock) each morning, baby-sits at least twice a week (all day) while his wife sells Avon. Our attendance has fallen off about 1/3 percent since he has been here. The offering has fallen off about 1/2 percent.

"Our church doesn't believe in running the preacher off, but in this situation I would vote for him to leave tomorrow. After all, a man that is too lazy to work, doesn't deserve to eat."

Obviously, there was more to the story. It appeared there had been a bad experience between this anonymous letter writer and the minister. But the letter writer was right about one thing. The church deserved to have a pastor whose manner and presence were not offensive.

The minister should be clean, practice good hygienic habits, and be sensitive to the personal expectations of the church.

I have formed a prejudice which is just that—a prejudice. Whether or not it has any bearing on the matter, I would not know. It appears to me that an inordinate number of the ministers who attend our Forced Resignation Workshops are overweight. Some are obese. If a church loves and affirms the minister, the church may not notice that he or she is obese. But if the church members develop a legitimate reason for being dissatisfied with the minister, they will notice. Obesity may become an issue since it suggests that the minister is compulsive. If he or she is compulsive in eating habits, carelessness in other matters may be a factor. It is hard to imagine a minister who "has it all together" emotionally and spiritually who "has it all out front" physically.

7. Potpourri

I have no good category for this last reason why churches become dissatisfied with ministers. Churches are as complex and complicated as nations. The expectations are wide and varied. Sometimes they make sense. Frequently, they do not make sense.

One group of church members became dissatisfied with a minister of youth because he drove an MGB. It is too symbolic of radicalism, they contended in the charges. One group in another church felt the minister of education developed too many cliques in the church. She did not minister to the entire congregation.

Church staff members can affect the mood and temperament of the congregation. Unknowingly, and undeliberately, staff members can create a mood of dissatisfaction with other staff members.

One letter we received about the article in a church-related periodical on forced resignation was from the wife of a staff member.

"For over fifteen years now, my husband and I have served in the ministry of music. I do not read extensively, but what I do read seems to be geared to the plight of the pastor. There never seems to be any consideration to the needs of the other staff members.

"In the church we now serve, our pastor has been given medical care, auto upkeep, membership to the country club, clothing, as well as salary and housing and other 'fringe benefits' that amount to over twice what my husband is paid. We are in a church of professional people and feel that we are expected to live in such a way so as not to embarrass the church.

"When the new pastor came almost a year ago, we had another church to go to, but through his insistence, we decided to stay here 'for the sake of the church.' Three months after his coming, he said, 'I am praying that God will lead you elsewhere.' Through pressure on the Minister to Senior Adults and the Minister to Youth from the pastor, these two have resigned. The Educational Director was 'fired' and given 60 days to leave."

In this situation, it appeared the mood and temperament of the congregation could have been affected by the church staff's interpersonal conflict. The pastor could create dissatisfaction with the other staff members. The staff members, could, in turn, create dissatisfaction with the pastor. The staff members might also create dissatisfaction with each other.

Still another factor is theological position. The minister may be too radical, too liberal, too conservative, or too moderate. It would be profitable for the minister to test the theological waters of the congregation to be sure he or she can be comfortable with the large majority of feelings.

The congregation should also be fair. If some theological

or biblical issues (not always the same) are of central importance to the congregation, these should be communicated to the prospective minister. For example, a church in Missouri had "split" over open or closed communion. One group believed in open communion, inviting any Christian to participate in the Lord's Supper when it is observed. The other group believed in closed communion, limiting the observance of the Lord's Supper to members only.

The "closed communion" group failed to communicate to their prospective pastor the intensity of their beliefs. When the issue came up some four months after calling the pastor, the minister was dismissed because he favored open communion.

When the ministers who attended the Forced Resignation Workshop in Denton, Texas were asked to isolate one central cause for the dissatisfaction of the congregation to the point of asking for their resignation, they responded:

"Opposition from the power structure in the church;
"The music director led a revolt;
"The staff averaged twenty years older than the pastor;
"Been there too long—twenty-five years is enough;
"Staff conflict;
"Racial issue—church would not accept blacks and Hispanics;
"Staff problem (mentioned six times);
"Power struggle (mentioned three times);
"Lack of financial leadership;
"The church wanted a new face;
"The founder of the church wanted me to leave;
"Torpedoed by three would-be pastors;
"Church was immature;
"Church was not concerned for winning the lost;
"Same old problem—this was the sixth church from which I was fired."

As mentioned earlier in the chapter, it is difficult, perhaps impossible, to isolate the exact reasons why churches become so dissatisfied with ministers that they force them to resign. This is a partial list at best. The reader will develop many more, and the reasons will be just as valid as these that have been listed.

Notes

1. Speed Leas, "A Study of Involuntary Terminations in Some Presbyterian, Episcopal, and United Church of Christ Congregations" (Washington, D.C.: The Alban Institute, Inc., 1980), p. 11.

2. Ibid., pp. 10-11.

3
Retraining:
The Ultimate Option

"What can we do? We have tried talking to him. We have discussed goals which are acceptable to him and to our committee. But these goals have been totally unacceptable to the congregation. What can we do?"

"What can I do? I have tried talking with the congregation. I have talked with the deacons. I have talked with the personnel committee. We have agreed upon goals, and I feel I have attained a sizable number of them. But I am still unhappy. My family is miserable. The church members act like they do not want me anymore. What can I do?"

Both sides feel helpless. But there is one ultimate option. Perhaps it will work. Why not provide for retraining for the minister *and* the church? That's right—*and* the church. This chapter is a strategy for retraining. This is the ultimate option for forced termination. When all else fails, retrain.

The retraining program we are recommending will not be easy. It could be expensive. But it is far better than opening wounds of a nature that may take decades to heal. Furthermore, it may be the most redemptive option available. It may help the church for years to come.

It is done for businesses and schools. When a personnel problem has reached an impasse, one of the most sensible options is to retrain the persons involved. The business or school profits. The persons involved become remotivated. And the most economical approach has been found. It can also work for churches.

1. The Gathering Storm in Ministerial Training

Several years ago, Jeffrey K. Hadden wrote *The Gathering Storm in the Churches*. In the book he suggested four crises that have gathered the storm. First, "The crisis of meaning and purpose." Laity and clergy alike are asking, Who are we? What are we about? We cannot drift on endlessly without direction. Second, "The crisis of belief." In this crisis Hadden feels laity and clergy are dealing with divisive opinions as to what constitutes appropriate belief. Third, "the crisis of authority." Neither clergy nor laity has clear understanding about where authority in the churches lies. The question of who's in charge may become of primary significance. Fourth, "The crisis of identity." Hadden feels this is a crisis of ministry. The minister is not sure who he is and how he fits into the whole schemata of the church.[1]

To these four Mark Rouch, in his stimulating work *Competent Ministry*, adds the "crisis of competence."[2] Colleges and seminaries do necessary and unequaled work. But they do not complete the task of training. The crisis of competence is sustained because the pilgrimage of growth never ends.

Both the church and the minister must recognize the crises and deal with them if they are to continue the work of redemption in their community.

All of us who work with the ongoing training of ministers and their families have heard the message: "I just was not prepared for this kind of church in seminary." But who is? No one, of course. Each church brings distinctive difficulties as well as possibilities. Each church will unveil the deficiencies in ministers so quickly that they will not know they have been derobed until their defense mechanisms are stripped and they stand emotionally naked.

Often the following happens. The minister begins the ministry in a church with a concept of what the mission and purpose of the church should be. To this setting, a belief system of the minister is brought to the church that has been developed through the minister's entire lifetime. Additionally, the minister has constituted a personal concept of authority. Most of this concept is enigmatic. Few ministers I have known intimately have a clear understanding of the authority structure in a church.

Like an electric bolt of lightning the storm erupts. The storm has gathered through the development of a naive minister thinking this is the way it ought to be. The church, meanwhile, is feeling manipulated and used because traditions have been ignored. When the resistance of the church is fought with guerrilla determination, the minister reaches crisis number 4: identity. He thinks, *Who in heaven's name am I? and what on earth am I doing here among this den of wolves? Foul! Foul!*

I agree with Rouch. Both sides must begin with competence, not just the minister. Certainly the minister must increase competence. But the church must do the same. There is a strategy for doing both.

2. How It Works!

The chairman of deacons has been getting calls daily. Some of the calls are from church members who enjoy a little dissension. They enjoy the stir. But some of the calls are from the levelheaded leaders. The pastor must be negotiated with soon. He keeps virtually no office hours. He cannot be reached by phone. He takes too many outside speaking engagements. He has alienated the largest financial contributor in the church. He feels no responsibility to the deacons. "So, John, since you are the chairman of deacons, what are you going to do about it?"

John knows the complaints are relative and varied. It is hard to get a handle on them because of their ambiguity. He makes an appointment with the pastor.

The meeting is awkward. John does not enjoy the role of being a heavy. The pastor, it seems to John, is threatened and defensive. But John presses on to work out a solution. He has been a member of this church since early childhood. His parents were raised in this church. He loves this church. The spiritual welfare of the church is a primary concern for him.

"Pastor, I am trying to find solutions. I am not here to create more problems," says John.

"I have always felt you had the interests of the church at heart," replied the pastor.

"What can we do?" asked John.

"Well, I feel the church needs to understand my role better. But I also admit that I could try to understand the church better. I suggest we work at trying to reach a mutual retraining program for both the church and me."

John and the pastor divided the training areas into five categories.

1. *The Mission of the Church*	1. *The Mission of the Pastor*
2. *Basic Biblical Beliefs of Church*	2. *Basic Biblical Beliefs of Pastor*
3. *Authority in the Church*	3. *Pastoral Authority*
4. *The Church Organization*	4. *Pastoral Organization*
5. *Spiritual Growth in the Church*	5. *Spiritual Growth of the Pastor*

A training program was designed.

It was agreed the deacons should be trained first in order to facilitate the training process for the entire church. A date was set for a retreat for the deacons. They would begin on Friday evening in a setting away from the church. They would conclude on Saturday afternoon with an outdoor hamburger cookout. The agenda and content were agreed upon.

Agenda for Retraining for Pastor and Deacons
(title: "Our Church Sharing the Ministry of Christ")

Friday

5:30 PM Registration and fellowship

6:00 PM Evening meal

7:00 PM Introduction of program, "Our Church Sharing the Ministry of Christ"

The chairman of deacons gives an overview of the weekend agenda. "Our Church Sharing the Ministry of Christ" is larger than any one person. If we are to be the church and do the work of the church, we must realize the strength which comes from sharing the total ministry of Christ. Jesus gave us a model. When He was preparing the disciples, He said, "A new commandment I give to you, that you love one another, even as I have loved you, that you also love one another. By this all men will know that you are My disciples, if you have love for one another" (John 13:34-35).

7:15 PM 1. The Mission of the Church

One church member who is familiar with the history of the church gives a consensus statement about the mission of the church. What church is to be and do should be central to this presentation. For example, in *The Baptist Faith and Message* Herschel H. Hobbs writes, "A New Testament Church is an autonomous body, operating through democratic process under the Lordship of Jesus Christ. In such a congregation members are equally responsible. Its Scriptural officers are pastors and deacons."[3]

1. The Mission of the Pastor

The pastor gives an overview of the mission of the pastor taken from 1 Timothy 3. He should show the relationship of the pastor to the deacons as given in the same chapter beginning in verse 8.

If your church has outlined the responsibilities and duties of the pastor and deacons, this would be an excellent time to review these.

The pastor leads the church as an "enabler." He enables the church to be more effective through outreach, missions, Bible teaching, training, music, and service. Share with your deacons "The Servant Church" led by the servant pastor. This concept is developed by Leonard Griffith in *We Have This Ministry*.[4]

1. A servant is someone who works in somebody else's house—God's house.

2. A servant is someone who ministers to somebody else's needs.

3. A servant is someone who works at somebody else's convenience.

4. A servant is someone who does not expect to be thanked.

The pastor and deacons are servants of God's people in God's house.

7:45 PM   Discussion of how the blend of the mission of the

church and the mission of the pastor can work together.

8:00 PM   Break
8:10 PM   Basic Biblical Beliefs of the Church
Ask one of the more scholarly deacons to give an overview of the basic beliefs of the church. He should have as resources the Bible, a concordance, a statement of the beliefs of your denomination,[5] and a copy of your church's constitution and by-laws.

8:30 PM   Basic Biblical Beliefs of the Pastor
The pastor should give an overview of theological beliefs based on the Scriptures. He should show how his beliefs fit into the total context of the church.

8:50 PM   Discussion of how the basic biblical beliefs of both church and pastor are a way of joining leadership which gives additional strength.

9:15 PM   Adjourn and fellowship

Saturday
7:00 AM   Breakfast
7:45 AM   Devotional led by one of the deacons
8:00 AM   Authority in the Church and Pastoral Authority
(Guest speaker)
Using the Scriptures and your church's statement on authority, the person leading this presentation should be an outside leader trusted by all persons attending. This person could do a biblical study of authority.
In most churches, the basic authority is the Bible. The biblical guide to authority gives sufficient evidence that the Scriptures are adequate

to meet the critical issues of any problem in the church.

During the last century, three distinct concepts of deacon authority have been evident in Baptist churches.

(1) Deacons as Board of Directors
    a. All recommendations are screened by the deacons before going to church business meeting.
    b. Pastor and staff are responsible to the deacons rather than to the church.
    c. All expenditures must first be approved by the deacons.

(2) Deacons as Business Managers
    a. Deacons' responsibilities are those of business management.
    b. Deacons administer affairs of the church primarily as a business operation.
    c. Deacons are the decision makers in most business affairs.

(3) Deacons Serving in Pastoral Ministries
    a. Deacons build and maintain Christian harmony and fellowship.
    b. Deacons proclaim through witnessing to believers and unbelievers.
    c. Deacons seek to meet needs through caring activities of counseling, encouragement, grief ministry, and guidance in crisis.

For further discussion, see *The Ministry of the Deacon* by Howard B. Foshee.[6]

The leader of this portion should be familiar with the book *The Doctrine of Biblical Authori-*

ty by Russell H. Dilday, Jr.[7] Chapter 8 is especially helpful to Southern Baptists.

9:00 AM Discussion by the entire group.

9:15 AM Break

9:30 AM The Church Organization and Pastoral Organization

In a Baptist church, for example, there are five program organizations: pastoral ministries, a church in Bible study and outreach, the missions program, the music program, and training program. (Use the book *A Dynamic Church* by W. L. Howse and W. O. Thomason as a major resource.[8])

The pastor and one deacon should team-teach this portion. An alternative would be to invite the guest speaker and the pastor to team-teach this portion. Four tasks are essential for pastoral organization: (1) proclaim; (2) engage in fellowship of worship, witness, educational ministry, and application; (3) lead the church in performing its tasks; and (4) care, which includes pastoral care and ministry to needs of the church and community.[9]

The deacons are a part of the pastoral ministries team in performing these tasks. The church is organized into the other program organizations and appropriate committes and services as needed.

Two additional resources that will help clarify this portion are *A Church on Mission* by Reginald M. McDonough and *Priorities in Ministry* by Ernest Mosley.[10]

10:30 AM Discussion

10:40 AM Spiritual Growth in the Church

Ask three deacons to answer the following questions:

(1) At what time in your life did God's grace become a reality more than a word?

(2) What one experience in your life helped you realize God's forgiveness?

(3) What two experiences in the life of your church made you realize that you wanted to be a part of this church?

11:15 AM Group Discussion

11:30 AM Spiritual Growth of the Pastor

Ask the pastor to deal with the following questions in his closing remarks:

(1) How did you feel about the call of this church to be their pastor?

(2) What two experiences stand out as spiritual highlights in the ministry to this church?

(3) In what ways has God helped you to grow as a person since beginning your ministry in this church?

12:00 AM Lunch

1:00 PM Wrap-up

In conclusion, the deacons and pastor will discuss the answers to the following questions:

(1) What can we do together to help our church get a better focus on the mission of Christ for our community?

(2) In what ways can we better pattern the life of Christ to the membership of our church?

(3) In what specific activities can we take the findings of this retreat back to the entire membership of our church? (Ask members of the deacon body to discuss ways that

visitation or training activities can help solidify the body of the church.)

(4) What can we do to resolve the differences and take advantage of the similarities of the ministry of the deacons and the pastor?

2:00 PM Adjourn

The agenda, when abbreviated, looks like this:

"Our Church Sharing the Ministry of Christ"
(Agenda for Retraining for Pastors and Deacons)

Friday
5:30 PM Registration and Fellowship
6:00 PM Evening Meal
7:00 PM Introduction
7:15 PM The Mission of the Church
7:30 PM The Mission of the Pastor
7:45 PM Discussion
8:00 PM Break
8:10 PM Basic Biblical Beliefs of the Church
8:30 PM Basic Biblical Beliefs of the Pastor
8:50 PM Discussion
9:15 PM Adjourn and Fellowship

Saturday
7:00 AM Breakfast
7:45 AM Devotional
8:00 AM Authority in the Church and Pastoral Authority
9:00 AM Discussion
9:15 AM Break
9:30 AM The Church Organization and Pastoral Organization
10:30 AM Discussion

10:40 AM Spiritual Growth of the Church
11:15 AM Discussion
11:30 AM Spiritual Growth of the Pastor
12:00 AM Lunch
 1:00 PM Wrap-up
 2:00 PM Adjourn

Now, a word especially for the chairman of deacons mentioned earlier in this chapter:

A good question, John, if you are taking your work as chairman of the deacons seriously, is, Why would we do this? What good would this retraining program for the deacons and pastor do? Also, have we really wrestled with the issue that we are having problems with the pastoral leadership?

Those are good questions, John. I want to try to deal with some good answers.

First, your church would never forgive itself if you did not give your best effort in trying to solve the problem in a positive way. This is a good option for trying to solve the problem in a positive way. It says, *We have given it our best shot.*

Second, a retreat will give a redemptive atmosphere to deal with a sensitive problem. Approaching the problem as if there were two sides shows effort on both parts. The deacons are trying to better understand the pastor. And the pastor is trying to better understand the church.

Third, you will be surprised how many delicate issues will be dealt with in an agenda similar to the one in this book. You will have an opportunity to deal with some tender issues in an objective way, in the spirit and manner of Christians.

One more good thing about this approach. It will provide a planning environment for looking to the future with hope and redemption. It will give some added incentive to deal with all the critical issues and avoid getting hung up in the issues of "What's wrong with our pastor?"

As a followup, you may arrange weekly or semiweekly opportunities for the deacons and pastor to get together and share their concerns about the church. Some of the best support groups in the church are those which have resulted from a crisis. Although it may sound a bit like Pollyanna to say so, some of the most productive accomplishments possible have come from crisis.

Notes

1. Jeffrey K. Hadden, *The Gathering Storm in the Churches* (New York: Doubleday and Company, 1969), pp. 1-33, 212-221.

2. Mark Rouch, *Competent Ministry* (Nashville: Abingdon Press, 1974), p. 36.

3. Herschel H. Hobbs, *The Baptist Faith and Message* (Nashville: Convention Press, 1971), pp. 74-82.

4. Leonard Griffith, *We Have This Ministry* (Waco: Word Books, 1973), pp. 51-56.

5. Almost all denominations have helps and resources in this area. For Southern Baptists, the tract "The Baptist Faith and Message" is available for a nominal fee from the Tract Editor, Baptist Sunday School Board, 127 Ninth Avenue, North, Nashville, Tennessee 37234. The Baptist Faith and Message is a statement adopted by the Southern Baptist Convention in 1963. It gives help in what most Baptists believe: the Scriptures, God, man, salvation, God's purpose of grace, the church, baptism and the Lord's Supper, the Lord's Day, the Kingdom, last things, evangelism and missions, education, stewardship, cooperation, the Christian and social order, peace and war, and religious liberty.

6. Howard B. Foshee, *The Ministry of the Deacon* (Nashville: Convention Press, 1968), pp. 32-37.

7. Russell H. Dilday, Jr., *The Doctrine of Biblical Authority* (Nashville: Convention Press, 1982).

8. W. L. Howse and W. O. Thomason, *A Dynamic Church* (Nashville: Convention Press, 1969).

9. Ibid., p. 36.

10. Reginald M. McDonough, *A Church on Mission* (Nashville: Convention Press, 1980) and Ernest Mosley, *Priorities in Ministry* (Nashville: Convention Press, 1978).

4

The Staff Member
Who Can't Cut It

by WILL BEAL

1. Identify the Whys

A. *Conflict with the Pastor*

No other business or organization deals more with people than the church. The church is in the people business. Differing values and skills of a team of ministers create an arena for conflict. In this setting, the possibility for conflict is heightened when the other church staff members forget that the pastor is the staff leader. There should be no competition for the position of pastor. It will be confusing to leadership and followers if there is not a leader. In my twenty years of serving churches as a minister of education, I wanted to be with a pastor who was a leader and would claim his leadership.

The pastor can translate successes of another minister on staff as a move toward being pastor. A staff minister must be sensitive to his or her own role. If an associate hopes to pastor someday, then the lines of responsibility should be clearly drawn. In my own ministry, I have worked a low profile with some pastors because I could overpower their personality—not their position. I have always tried to send the message to the pastor that I had no desire to be pastor. I am a minister of education called, prepared, and committed to the ministry of education. I was to assist my pastor in ministry.

Conflict will call for confrontation. Why is it so difficult to confront? Some ministers would do almost anything to avoid confronting another staff member. A pastor may avoid confronting a staff member with bad news. In contrast, most pastors will welcome the chance to share good news with the staff member. Conflict cannot be resolved until resistance to confrontation is faced and overcome.

The fear of confrontation for the staff leader comes from four other identifiable fears.

(1) *The fear of discomfort.* A pastor is a caring person, or he couldn't be a minister. His caring instinct may become a liability when it comes to confrontation. No pastor gets a thrill from assisting in the dismissal of another staff member. It hurts.

(2) *The fear of reprisal* by the confronted person is a deterrent to confrontation. In business it is said, "Never be unkind to a subordinate; he may become your boss someday." In ministry this seldom happens unless in one of our state or convention offices. There is the impact of the thought, "What could this action do to my future career?"

(3) *Fear of denial.* The staff member accused may deny all, and this leaves the pastor in the position of getting material witnesses or having factual proof. "Can I substantiate my claim?" is a question that needs to be considered before charges are made.

(4) *The fear of consequences.* What if the word gets out that we had to ask the staff member to leave because he is homosexual? Think of the repercussions. Did we look into his character before we called him? Who were his friends while he was here? How will this reflect on the church? Pastors will experience much stress as they try in a redemptive way to dismiss a staff member on moral behavior.

B. Creating Own Church Within a Church

Any interest group created within the church should have as its purpose the strengthening and doing of the ministry of the church. A church is a church. It is not a music program, Sunday School, missionary organizations, youth work, worship services, or even evangelism; it is all of these. The minister of education, through the organizations, will touch the lives of most people in a church. This is not cause to separate any activity from the mission of the church. There can be no priority organization in a church. There are only priority needs that need to be met through a church's ministries.

Church organizations may get center stage because the church has not stated its purpose. If a church will work through its church council or long-range planning committee to do priority planning, the church's ministries can direct efforts toward a common goal.

A church within a church is created and sustained around a personality or personalities under the guise of a church organization. Its purpose is to emphasize its leadership while robbing the church of strength and witness. The best deterrent of self-interest groups is through joint planning and budget control. Any program that will use time, money, people, or physical resources should be studied and approved within the church council. And the council is guided by the stated objectives of the church.

While I was serving as a minister of education, our minister of youth came to me requesting the money to take the youth on a trip to the Northeast. As presented it sounded good and worthy, but the church council turned down the request because it made little or no contribution to the church's stated priorities. Of course, there will be maverick end runs with great special events if no game plan is adopted by the team.

C. Pastor Wants His "Own People"

A great fear of staff members is "When the pastor leaves, where does that leave me?" Should staff members resign when the pastor does, or should they resign when a new pastor comes, or should they resign at all? I have found it helpful to go back and look at my call. My call to the ministry was from the Lord, but what was my call to this church? Was I called by a pastor, a committee, or a congregation, and how was the Lord working in my call? The staff member who is dismissed will really replay these tapes. If staff members are called, how do they get uncalled? To answer my own question—"A call is not dissolved; it is replaced with another call."

If a new pastor wants to bring in his own team, how can this be done and respect the call of those already on the staff? Will he negate the call of others? In my opinion it is unethical for a new pastor to indiscriminately replace the present staff with his favorites. All staff ministers must be cautious not to manipulate the call to meet their own human desires.

A pastor needs to accept the "on board" staff of a church as a part of his call to that church. He should make the opportunity as a prospective pastor to talk eye to eye and heart to heart with the on board staff and try to determine if their approaches to ministry will "mesh" or "mash."

At one church where I served we changed pastors and before the new pastor came, I told him I would be leaving. It was an understanding we had before he came. I stayed three months after he came to help him and to finish my work. It was a healthy and mutual agreement. But that agreement only came about because we didn't play games; we discussed our own desires in ministry with openness and respect. This is a very sensitive time in the lives of ministers, and the greater percentage make the transition with integrity.

2. What Is the Church's Responsibility?

How does the church look at the calling of its ministers? Is the pastor's call different from the other staff ministers, and if so—how? A church may say, We call our pastor and the other staff ministers are employed. Or the staff manager may be given a budget out of which he can hire and fire as he wishes. I had a pastor hand me a piece of paper saying, "Just write down what you want as a salary." That was fun but scary because I knew he could easily tell me to pack my bags. The wise pastor will educate the people as to how God's will is at work in the calling of all ministers.

> Extending a call to a staff member involves more than employment. Basically it involves an earnest effort to follow divine leadership in finding the right person for each staff position. A church should earnestly pray before seeking to locate the proper person for each leadership responsibility. In this way the church will not make the mistake of simply asking God to bless its efforts in finding someone. Also, prayer will keep the church from simply "hiring" a staff member when it should be seeking to find God's will in choosing a leader for a divinely appointed task.[1]

Ministers need to feel security in ministry, and a fellowship of caring believers can do much to offer this to its ministers. Security for the minister is:

> Freedom from undue concern about financial income
> Feeling of comfort where you are
> Healthy self-esteem
> Confident of being in God's will
> Having a salable skill
> Support from significant others.

A trained personnel committee can help make its ministers feel more secure and happy in ministry. The personnel committee can request and administrate such benefits as:

insurance, vacation, sabbatical leave, monies for continued education and personal library, etc. These will cost the church very little extra and can add greatly to the morale of its staff.

What is the church's responsibility in dismissing a staff member? Our churches need to learn how to release a staff member. One year while at Glorieta I spoke with a young minister of education who was having difficulty. He had come to Glorieta and brought some of the Sunday School leadership. While he was at Glorieta his position was declared vacant and he had only a check waiting for him when he got home. He was in shock when he called me. There are times when a church needs to release a minister, but it needs to be done with dignity. Churches become known in the area and Convention for their treatment of their staff. Uncaring leaders in a congregation can project a negative image for the whole church. How does the congregation feel about a situation when a staff member is forced to resign?

Churches need a written policy on the calling and the dismissing of all staff members. Most churches will have policies and procedures on how they call and dismiss the pastor, but not the complete minister staff. There may be a statement on the calling of a minister of education but no statement on how to dismiss that person. If it will take church action to call a staff member, then why not have such a policy for dismissal? Staff members and church members need policies and procedures.

The personnel committee should be ultimately responsible for dismissing a staff member. A pastor needs the protection of the committee in dismissing procedures involving another minister. A staff manager should use the direct approach in dealing with a staff member who is not making it. A supervisor is obligated to explain why a salary increase is not given. Written messages should be avoided. Performance reviews by the staff manager and/or personnel committee will be a preventive measure. Growing, healthy ministers will want to know where they are falling short and will welcome suggestions on how to correct their course.

3. "I Don't Want to Go Through That Again"

Few things in life are as traumatic as being dismissed (fired) from a church staff. As a young man just out of the seminary I was fired from my first full-time church. We had two young boys and were hundreds of miles from our homes. With a small severance pay my family and I headed back to the Southwest to live six months with my wife's folks. During those six months out of ministry, I experienced anger, bitterness, and even thoughts of revenge. I questioned my call, considered other types of employment, and carried a burden of uselessness. The caring love of my wife and the innocent love of my two children helped me survive.

Again, I went back to my call and through the struggle God assured me that He has extended to me a divine invitation to be His minister. The wound has healed, but there is still a scar. From that experience I will always have a great sensitivity for the rejected person who is called of God.

The minister's first response to being dismissed is disbelief. How could this happen to me? I have given my life to the Lord, I have prepared for ministry, I have been obedient to His call. Why? This feeling is followed by bitterness. Hurt generates bitterness. Then comes a feeling of alienation. One thinks, *I am not what I wanted to be, so those who are—will they look down on me or even reject me?* This feeling may lead to self-alienation.

In ministry, there is high commitment. Ministers are called. Choice of ministry is known to all the kinfolk and neighbors. Mother proudly says to her mother, "Did you know Billy is going to be a minister?" And we unreservedly pledge our allegiance to our profession, even to the point that for us to pull out of the ministry would be a great disappointment to many.

The family involvement in ministry is deeper than in most professions. When a staff member is called to a place of service, the whole family is involved. When a minister is fired, the whole family is fired.

We are caring people. Ministers are compliant people desiring to please, which makes us more subject to hurt. We rely much on acceptance and the opposite, rejection, can be devastating.

Dismissal can be the best thing to happen to your career. Dismissal can be an occasion for growth.

4. How Can the Minister Prevent Dismissal?

A minister must claim responsibility for his/her destiny. I saw an interesting plaque the other day in a department store. It said, "God Blesses this House—But He Doesn't Clean It." It reminded me of the human/divine; both are at work in ministry. Ministry is a partnership with God. We cannot blame God or self for our failure (unless we have blatantly committed sin) or our success; we work together with God. God blesses ministry, but people do it.

If there is a repeated pattern of short tenure, if we are thinking others are always wrong, if we are unrealistic in our expectations of others, or if we are just plain lazy, then we may need some counseling about our career choice.

Let's look at some very practical measures we could take to possibly prevent forced resignation.

A. Keep Yourself Marketable
Whether we like it or not, we need to think, "What salable skill do I have that a church should pay me a salary for?" We stay marketable by:

      Being productive—work hard, be a growth agent
      Being dependable—be on time, pay your bills

Being a team member—give and take, join the team
Being known—make friends, do association work

B. Work with Options

This doesn't mean go into ministry with an out. But you need to consider what you could do to make a living if you were not in the ministry. I have a son who felt God's call to ministry. While he was in college I urged him to get a teaching certificate at the same time. Eighteen months after graduation he and his wife divorced. Later he said, "Now I hear what you were saying."

C. Continue to Grow

In commencement exercises a diploma is awarded. It is just a start, a commencing, a beginning of a career and an education. We need to continue to educate ourselves. Personal and professional growth has little to do with age or intelligence; self-determination and worth are more important. We need to challenge ourselves to reach beyond what is comfortable. Chart where you want your career to go. Those who succeed in ministry are those who clearly define their goals and habitually direct their energies in that direction.

D. Go Planning to Stay

The first thing I look at on a resumé is not age or education but the tenure pattern. With God's help, we need to select a place of service where we can invest ourselves in the people and the community. Begin to think of service in five-year blocks. It takes one year to say hello to a congregation, three years to know how to do your better work, and five years to have a track record. Think five, ten, fifteen, or twenty years in a church.

E. *Take on the Role of a Servant*

Taking on the servant role and being comfortable in it is a way of earning the respect you want. Christ exemplified a desire to serve: "The Son of Man came not to be served but to serve" (Matt. 20:28, RSV).

F. *Boost the Pastor*

Be the pastor's best cheerleader. Be devoted; earn his trust. Join up with a pastor you can love and give your allegiance to. Don't play games with him. Be honest. Keep him informed about what your program plans are. Remember, many pastors are still learning how to share their ministry.

5. What Can the Staff Member Forced to Resign Do?

A. *Respond to the Dismissing Group*

Ask to meet with them to negotiate for some time. It is very difficult to move to another church from no church. Try to stay; ask for time to make a move. A church should give a staff minister at least six months to move. Most churches want to save themselves embarrassment, as does the person involved. Be cautious; it is human to vent your anger by leaving too quickly. An "I'll show them" attitude always makes you the loser.

B. *Ask for Help*

Some of us find it difficult to admit we need help from others. Just sharing will take some of the pressure off. We are not superpersons; we are ministers. We cry, too. Ask the church or pastor for a letter of recommendation. This is very important. Don't let your pride make you look foolish by refusing to ask for help. Many times the pastor can act as your broker.

C. Don't Seek Revenge

It's a temptation to strike back at the church somehow, if that's who we blame for our dismissal. We know there are neurotic churches just as there are neurotic people. The church with all its warts still belongs to the Lord, and it is the extension of Jesus Christ into today's world. It was an act of compassion when I was asked to resign from my first church, although I did not know it then. When a minister-friend is forced to resign and seems consumed by a negative spirit, we need to reach out to him rather than avoid him. Our sensitivity and understanding will help him.

D. Look Before You Leap

Ministers need to do better courting before they marry themselves to a church. Investigate the church and its staff before signing on board. Consult with your mate. Match your personality with the personality of a church. Talk with past staff members of a prospective church to see how they felt about their ministry. You cannot know all about a church or staff before you go to a church. Gather information, sift through it, and ask the Lord for wisdom in your consideration.

Christ Himself was rejected by the religious leaders of His day. He was betrayed by a chosen disciple and was denied by His best friend. Christ found security because He was doing the will of His Father, because He had a definite mission to accomplish, and because He exhibited a positive and redemptive spirit.

Note
1. W. L. Howse, *The Church Staff and Its Work* (Nashville: Broadman Press, 1959), p. 26.

5

What to Consider
If an Impasse Is Reached

If the church has given its best efforts to resolve the problem, what should be considered? If the minister or the church has drawn the lines of "no movement," what is the next step? This chapter concedes the fact that there are times when an impasse is reached. There are times when some action, painful though it may be, must be taken.

1. Use the Biblical Model

Matthew 18:15-17 and 2 Corinthians 2:4-8 are the two passages which should be sought in using the biblical model when an impasse is reached.

It should be noted that in 2 Corinthians 2:4-8, the recommended discipline was grounded in love. The mood of the discipline was reclamation. Positive fellowship was confirmed in love. And, most importantly, "It was the congregation which exercised the discipline."[1]

Most churches which have Christian discipline written into their structure have provisions of some form of excommunication for those members "who are guilty of notorious and atrocious crimes."[2] If the minister is guilty of a notorious and atrocious crime, the church has little choice but to terminate the relationship. If the minister is embarrassing the church through sins against the Ten Commandments,

the church should treat the offender in the biblical manner
suggested in Matthew 18 and 2 Corinthians 2. If the sins are
highly scandalous in nature and expose the church to con-
tempt, then the church should first seek repentance from
the minister, and then provide for the next redemptive step
to benefit the church as well as the minister.

In applying the biblical model, remember that *nowhere* in
the New Testament can the mechanical application of a set
of rules be proven. The manner was always one of seeking
repentance and reclamation. To maintain the sense of dignity and authority of the church, the first order of application of the biblical model should be that of love. The model
of the love of Christ should be primary.

2. Some Indispensable Questions to Ask Before Action

Some factors must be dealt with before ultimatums are
given.

(1) Is the minister a disturbed person?

If he or she is disturbed, this person should be treated in
the same way that you would treat a member of your family
who was disturbed.

How can you know? A disturbed person *distorts reality.*
He may have severe and unmanageable stress or anxiety. A
practical way of testing this highly technical disorder is to
observe behavior. Ask, is this behavior consistent to the
previous history? If the behavior is distorted and alarming-
ly inconsistent, take the next logical step. Get professional
help for the minister. Display the compassion of Christ by
offering to assist the person in getting help. He or she may
show anger and frustration but, in the long run, will have
been helped.

One of the more common forms of distortion is called
paranoia. This happens when a person feels the world is out
to get him or her. All persons have a little paranoia at one
time or another in their lives. But when it becomes an

obsession, it is past the normal neurosis of everyday living. It needs attention. Paranoid persons cannot or will not assume responsibility for the unsettling events around them. It is always someone else's fault. If a person cannot assume some of the responsibility in a conflict, you should have some apprehension about the person's ability to deal with reality. Usually when no responsibility for conflict is taken, the reality has already been distorted.[3]

Another form of distortion is *depression*. There are two kinds of depression. Acute depression is the result of some critical event in life, like the death of a family member. The characteristics are common. Quietness, lack of joy, inability to concentrate, loss of appetite, and unwillingness or inability to communicate are only a few. The second kind of depression is chronic, which has much the same characteristics. The difference is that chronic depression often occurs without any apparent cause. If the minister is a victim of either acute or chronic depression, this person needs help and support. The last thing this person needs is discipline for actions and behavior which cannot be controlled.

Still another form of distortion of reality is the "out of control" behavior. One of the more common "out of control" behaviors is overly aggressive behavior. For example, if a minister has been hurt by what he judges as unjust behavior, one of the symptoms of normal reaction is overly aggressive behavior: the "I'm gonna get them one way or another" behavior. This person will distort reality. A nice, polite, and gentle person may have fits of rage. Schmidt calls this person a "walking time bomb."[4]

One minister of education in a Western state was released from his work because he had "out of control" behavior. One Monday morning, in a church staff meeting, he had a disagreement with the pastor. The minister of education stood and invited the pastor outside to "settle the issue like men." When the pastor refused, he began breaking things in the office where the staff was meeting. A few weeks later, he challenged the chairman of the personnel committee to the same fisticuffs. After the church had taken action to release him, they found that he had been dishonorably discharged from the military service for just such an incident with an officer.

When the pastor was telling the story, he suggested that some preventive maintenance should have been taken to avoid the ugly showdown with the minister of education. In the first place, they had not checked his background. He had told them he was a retired sergeant major in the army and had been honorably discharged. He had not served a church before, but the church had not bothered to search out his background because he had been a member of the church. Too, they had not bothered to talk with his wife and family. They found out later that the family would have been more than willing to talk to them but was physically afraid of the husband and father. Later, the man was hospitalized for attacking his wife.

One of the first questions the church must ask is, Is the minister a disturbed person? If the answer is yes, then certain redemptive steps should be taken before the drama of ultimatum is drawn.

(2) Has the church prayed for a solution?

Prayer will solve problems. The prayer itself cannot. But God's answer to the prayer can. The resolution for solution that comes by praying is healing both for the church and the minister. Paul wrote in Colossians 4:2, "Devote yourselves to prayer, keeping alert in it with an attitude of thanksgiving." Be thankful for the positive contributions already made by the minister.

There is a powerful admonition in James 5:15 that should be heard. "And the prayer offered in faith will restore the one who is sick, and the Lord will raise him up, and if he has committed sins, they will be forgiven him."

Leaders of the church should call the church to prayer if the minister appears to be in danger of causing damage to the spiritual nature of the church.

(3) Has the church practiced the Spirit of Christ?

Paul wrote to the church at Thessalonica, "And we urge you, brethen, admonish the unruly, encourage the fainthearted, help the weak, be patient with all men. See that no one repays another with evil, but always seek after that which is good for one another and for all men" (1 Thess. 5:14-15).

If the minister is disturbed, there is all the more reason why the church should approach the minister with calmness, forgiveness, and faith. Such compassion will preserve the self-worth and dignity of the church. It is possible that the church can be a spiritual teacher for the minister.

Get help. Find ways to help the minister through a physician, counselor, or mentor. Help the minister find that he or she is in a church that cares for human beings. The lingering aftertaste of this kind of behavior for the church can be redemptive for years.

(4) Did we have this problem of dissension and conflict before the minister came?

One of the factors revealed by other studies of forced resignations in churches is that the problem in the church existed before the minister came. The church is full of people with integrity and compassion. These persons will help the church honestly look at this possibility. The church will then give serious consideration to the possibility with the leadership of these persons. If the problem is not in the minister's person or leadership, then the church might want to look elsewhere for the answer to the problem.

(5) Is the minister suffering symptoms of burnout?

Burnout is not a symptom of a disturbed person. Rather, it is a symptom of someone who is working through a par-

ticularly difficult time of stress in his or her life. The symptoms can be recognized by a caring church.

Are there signs of exhaustion? Has the spirit of joy been
missing in the minister's life? Does he or she appear to be
tired much of the time? Has the routine of work for the
minister changed dramatically during the past few weeks or
months? Does he or she appear to be more irritable? Is
delegation a problem? Does the minister appear to be doing
more of the work himself or herself? Is there weariness
apparent?

These are questions which become even more significant
if the minister is an overachiever. If the previous work
habits of the minister have been "go-go-go" and "do-do-do"
and now have become "whoa," "no," and "slow," then it is
time for the church to consider the possibility of burnout.

The minister should be given the same consideration a
church member is given. If burnout is a possibility, practice
patience. Look with compassion on the change in behavior
rather than looking with judgment. Most overachievers pull
themselves out of the symptoms of burnout. Sometimes
they need help. But most doldrums of persons who take life
seriously are natural and predictable.

The fact is that most creative persons have periods of
drought and burnout in their lives. If the minister is apa-
thetic by behavior, the dramatic change will not be noticed.
But if the minister is creative and effective in leadership,
somewhere and sometime in his ministry, this minister will
suffer some of the symptoms of burnout.

Not only patience, but *encouragement* should be given.
Paul needed Barnabas because he encouraged him in his
ministry. Ministers spend most of their time acting as a
Barnabas to the church. But ministers need a Barnabas, too.
In every congregation I have been in, someone has acted the
role of Barnabas for me. It is true that some ministers are
more approachable than others. Some ministers have diffi-

culty in revealing signs that they need encouragement, but all of them do need encouragement.

In addition to patience and encouragement, one other pattern of assistance to the minister should be practiced. That pattern is *direction*. The minister often has trouble taking advice. This, too, is natural. After all, the minister spends a great deal of his or her life giving advice. It is difficult to take advice.

In a church in Jackson, Mississippi, a man became chairman of the personnel committee whose work in his vocation was also in personnel. He was accustomed to suggesting to persons who needed improvement to get additional training. The minister was having some difficulty with the staff. Although the difficulty had two sides, the personnel committee chairman suggested that one of the alternatives to improvement should be that the pastor get some additional feedback on his leadership style.

The pastor attended a personal and professional growth course in Nashville, Tennessee. The program is designed to give sensitive feedback on the style of leadership of the minister. His first few days were spent in dealing with the anger he had with the chairman of the personnel committee. The pastor had been in the church for more than twenty years. The church had grown significantly. The staff had grown with the church. The pastor had been effective in his leadership. He gave off signals that he was embarrassed that a member of his church had to tell him that he needed some feedback. Although the pastor agreed that he needed help, it was still difficult to receive help that was suggested by a member of his church.

The story did have a happy ending. After working through his anger and embarrassment, the pastor then received some much-needed and valuable help. He later confided that he was glad he got some direction. Even though he probably would not have gotten the additional training without direction, the direction was still hard to digest.

Henry Adams wrote, "Too long has a pastor been regarded as learned because he has had extensive training. He is learned only if he is continually learning. Some of his most important learning comes only after ordination. His most vital theological education will be what he learns in the continuing present, all his mature years."[5]

The pastor who is suffering from symptoms of burnout needs direction. Often this direction can only come from the church.

(6) Does the minister have personal problems?

Although this question has overtones from (1) Is the minister a disturbed person? and (5) Is the minister suffering symptoms of burnout? there is still singular importance to asking if the minister has personal problems.

FAMILY. Is the minister having personal problems with his or her family? Is the spouse supportive? A minister's spouse is a team part of the ministry. True, the spouse is not necessarily called to ministry. But if the spouse if not giving support to the other team member, the minister will feel the lack of support. The church will be able to detect this.

Although the situation is infrequent, occasionally the minister or spouse gets involved in another relationship. It is impossible for a spouse to support the moral model of ministry for the minister if he or she is involved in an immoral relationship with another person. If the minister is involved in an immoral relationship, the church is obligated to deal with the situation. Although this does not always mean forced resignation, the church is responsible for dealing with the problem redemptively for the minister, the minister's family, and the church.

Children can be a problem for the minister. If the children cause an inordinate amount of anxiety, the minister's work will be affected. If a child is involved in unwed pregnancy, a minister usually asks, What did I do wrong? A church can help. A church can support the minister through this difficult time. Much of the guilt can be dealt with by caring church members. If a child of the minister gets involved in drugs, the church can help by dealing with the problem as caring and compassionate persons.

From 1977 to 1979 a research project was conducted by Dr. Tommy Dalton Bledsoe, as partial fulfillment of a Ph.D. The study was of 386 names of ministers whose resignations were reported (without references to relocation in new pastorates). The first of the major four conclusions Dr. Bledsoe reached was "Marital and/or familial tensions are present in varying degrees within most families of Southern Baptist ministers who undergo the career crisis of a loss of the pastorate, despite the supportiveness which wells up within the family."[6]

I suspect that many of the tensions were present even before the loss of the pastorate. This is not to say that these tensions were the cause of the loss of the pastorate. On the contrary, the tensions are dealt with in many families. They are dealt with constructively. But often these tensions can be contributing factors. The church should ask, Is the family a part of the cause of the difficulties we are having with the minister? If so, what can the church do to help?

ENTRANCE OR EXIT. The first three to five years of ministry are difficult for most ministers. The head is still full of theology. The heart is still full of unfulfilled dreams. The hands are itching to "do" church work. But almost all training has to be tempered with wisdom and experience. If ministry does not go as expected, the entrance years can be overpoweringly frustrating. If the enthusiasm of entrance is dampened, effectiveness will be affected. A church needs to be especially sensitive to the needs of the youthful minister.

Exit or preretirement years in ministry are also frequently difficult. The fear of being "turned out to pasture" is real. Studies have shown that most churches prefer youthful ministers. If a church begins to plan for a youthful minister before the minister retires, the exit years can consist of the minister asking, "Was I of any worth? Do they appreciate me? Where did my life go?" If this is true, then the church will begin to behave in uncharacteristic ways. These kinds of personal problems can affect the ministry in the church. A compassionate church will tune in to the possibility of these problems of entrance or exit and act accordingly. A compassionate church will not act impulsively as the result of complaints of some members who will not understand or sympathize with exit or entrance into ministry.

AMBITION. At times in the ministry of a person who takes the work seriously, the problem of ambition will come up. It may be a recurring problem rather than a one-time problem. Eventually, a minister goes through a "make it or break it" stage.[7] The minister will ask, How am I doing in relation to Bill and Jean who lived next door in Fuller Hall in seminary? Am I being passed by? Are other churches with more opportunities ignoring me? Why?

These kinds of questions create doubts. Self-esteem is at stake. The church also has to deal with a difficult problem. The problem for the church is the possibility of rejection. Like a jilted lover, the church may be tempted to say, If he doesn't care any more about us than that, then let him go. We'll help him go. But when these thoughts are considered rationally and more objectively, what industrious person has not gone through some of them? Again, the church should be admonished to be patient. Be careful not to overcompensate. This is the minister's problem. The church can help, but the church cannot solve the problem for the minister.

MID-CAREER CRISIS. Volumes have been written on the subject. Mid-career crisis may have all the previous personal problems rolled into one. But the minister goes through life cycles just as do church members. The inability to perform physically becomes paramount in the mind of a person who has heavy expectations of self.

In mid-career the minister needs the support of peers and loved ones. The minister must learn that effectiveness comes with experience and wisdom as well as with youthful enthusiasm and strength. If the minister is unable to get feedback from those who love him or her, it is easy to forget this essential fact.

SALARY FAIRNESS. Most ministers are not greedy or "money-grubbing" people who want something for nothing. Occasionally, that complaint can be heard from persons who are having trouble getting along with the minister. But, contrary to that notion, ministers are usually very fair in salary expectations.

But fairness means they expect to be treated as persons of worth. They should be paid equitable salaries. It is not always easy to establish what is equitable, but there are enough wise leaders in most churches to determine what is equitable. Indeed, most Baptist churches try hard to be fair and equitable in salaries of ministers. There are exceptions, but these are not the rule.

In a workship for ministers who had been forced to resign, one minister told the group, "I should've known it was inevitable during the last three years of my ministry when I wasn't given a raise." With the cost of living going up annually, this was equal to a minimum of a 20 percent cut in salary. Now, some churches cannot afford raises for the minister. Some churches have had such decreases in giving that raising the minister's salary would be detrimental to the economic stability of the church. Again, in most cases, ministers are mature enough to know when this is necessary. But if a refusal to increase the salary of the ministry is simply a punitive maneuver, it would be more honest to deal with the minister straight. What is going on? The minister has a right to know. The church has an obligation to be aboveboard. Salary discipline is hardly ethical without just cause.

Some church-related organizations have suggested salary structures for ministers. These structures are based on studies of churches of all different sizes and situations. A median range for your church is a good place to begin considerations for what is equitable.

Let us summarize these indispensable questions for a church to consider before taking the ultimate action of requesting forced resignation:

(1) Is the minister a disturbed person?
(2) Has the church prayed for a solution?
(3) Has the church practiced the Spirit of Christ?
(4) Did we have this problem of dissension and conflict before the minister came?
(5) Is the minister suffering symptoms of burnout?
(6) Does the minister have personal problems?

Family	Mid-Career Crisis
Entrance or Exit	Salary Fairness
Ambition	

A caring and compassionate church can save itself years of aftermath of guilt and shame by dealing with the issues above. These should be dealt with carefully before ultimatums are suggested or reached.

3. But Still No Solution?

Suppose all the questions in the last section have been dealt with constructively, and there still is no solution. What can the church do? Here are some positive steps to take if the impasse seems impassable.

(1) Call in a mediator.

Find someone trusted by both the minister and the church. Ask the mediator to hear both sides and offer some suggestions. The old adage "If you're too close to the trees you can't see the forest" applies. Someone needs to see the whole picture. A mediator can give objectivity to a volatile situation.

Remember, it is essential that the mediator be someone whom both sides trust. If an ally of either side is called in, matters could be made worse.

Who should the mediator be? Frequently, a director of missions or other church official can give objectivity. The church-minister relations director in a state can offer wisdom. A state convention official familiar with the church is another possible person to serve as mediator.

Avoid former pastors of the church or ministers who have more than a passing interest in the church. There is a strong possibility that the minister will have a built-in resistance to this person even if the church does not.

Although admittedly debatable, it is my opinion that a neutral place should be selected. If the place is neutral, the atmosphere will tend to be more neutral and fair for all. Find a convenient conference room in a nearby motel or school. Use another church. But avoid, if possible, the meeting ground where some battles may have been fought or, at least, brewed.

(2) Establish agreed-upon ground rules for the negotiations.

Work with the mediator to establish some ground rules for both sides. For example:

• Give both sides equal time in expressing views.

• Use the instrument of prayer as a request for help from God as opposed to teaching a moral lesson to either side.

• Establish a stopping time. You may need more than one or two meetings. Extended negotiation in the first meeting rarely solves problems. Frequently what is needed is more processing time. This avoids panic on either side. It also avoids having persons become so emotionally involved that the perspective of possible solution is lost.

• Avoid face-offs. A face-off occurs when one or both sides become so angry that ultimatums are the only option. Grown men with mature positions in life can be seduced into a "I dare you to knock this chip off my shoulder" position. Be sure to avoid this critical posture if at all possible.

• Ask both sides for possible solutions. A good question to be asked is, What can I do to solve the problem of this impasse?

• Ask the mediator to summarize the findings. In addition, he or she should make recommendations for additional meetings if necessary.

In advance of the meeting, the ground rules which have been agreed upon by both sides should be circulated to all persons who will have part in the meeting. These persons should be asked to contribute additional ground rules.

(3) Give Christ room to heal.

In dissension that has reached this level, there are no innocent parties. Usually the impasse has reached such proportions that mistakes have been made on both sides. Remember to give Christ room to heal.

These are decent human beings involved in a difficult situation. No one wants to lose face. Everyone should be afforded dignity. Everyone's opinion should be taken seriously. Avoiding put-downs is essential to the unity of reaching a solution. This is a Christlike way to search for healing.

Nothing soothes quite so much as a simple, "I could be wrong." Nothing compliments the humanity and dignity of another more than a simple, "You could be right." Paul wrote, "And be kind to one another, tender-hearted, forgiving each other, just as God in Christ also has forgiven you" (Eph. 4:32).

(4) Avoid secret meetings.

If the negotiations have begun for solving the problem,

avoid secret meetings. Secret meetings are usually a strategy for building a case. Most ministers are highly threatened by secret meetings. The church owes the minister the diplomacy and dignity of being straight.

Secret meetings are a platform for insinuations which may or may not have truth. People feel much more comfortable sharing a half-truth in a secret meeting than they do when the accused is present.

(5) Keep everyone informed.

The opposite side of avoiding secret meetings is keeping everyone informed. Keep the procedure for your plans open. This will afford fairness to all.

One minister in Missouri shared with a group of persons in a workshop that he went to Arizona for a two-week vacation. Within an hour after his return, the chairman of deacons met him at the parsonage. He informed the pastor that the deacons had met on Tuesday after he left on Monday and had voted to request his resignation. On the following Wednesday night the church was informed that a vote would be taken on Sunday morning immediately following the morning worship services. This was the procedure called for in the constitution and by-laws of the church. The church then voted by a two-thirds majority for his termination.

The distraught pastor asked for the charges. Some felt he had been there too long (three years). Others felt he did not visit the church members enough. Still others did not respect his leadership.

When the pastor asked why the church had not given him an opportunity to respond to these charges, the chairman replied that the church felt it would be best for all if the matter was not discussed with the pastor until action was taken.

Although we heard only one side of this story, if the procedure followed was accurate as the pastor implied, the church was led through a series of most unfortunate circumstances. As a human being, the pastor was entitled to hear the charges before they were brought before the church for a vote. (Even the church was not allowed the privilege of discussion.) The topic was brought before the church as a matter of course that the deacons knew what was best for the church. Not only does this violate the principles of a democratic process; it violates the rights of a human being. As painful as it may be, a church should keep everyone informed about the decision-making process, and every member should be allowed input.

A church should inform both members and pastor what the prerequisite steps for forced termination are. A body of leaders, deacons in this case, should not presume to act for the entire church on an issue as sensitive as forced termination.

In the next chapter, we will consider some caring ways for the church to consider the forced termination of a minister. Assuming that, after all efforts have been tried, the church still feels it best for all concerned that the minister be forced to terminate, the action in the steps should be compassionate. The next chapter is about how to take those steps.

Notes

1. Duke K. McCall, ed., *What Is the Church?* (Nashville: Broadman Press, 1958), p. 166.

2. Ibid., p. 180.

3. See Paul F. Schmidt, *Coping with Difficult People* (Philadelphia: Westminster Press, 1980), pp. 38-47. Schmidt feels that the person who is paranoid to the point of being disturbed displays characteristics of suspicion, arrogant accusation, and relentless blaming.

4. Ibid., p. 65.

5. Henry Adams as quoted by Charles William Steward, *Person and Profession* (Nashville: Abingdon Press, 1974), p. 124.

6. Tommy Dalton Bledsoe, "Case Studies of Georgia Baptist Ministerial Families Who Have Resigned Pastorates Without Immediate Prospects for Another Pastorate," Georgia State University, Atlanta, Georgia, 1980.

7. Steward, p. 76.

6
Steps to Take
to Terminate

In the previous chapter, we considered some things vital to the consideration of action. In this chapter the assumption is that action must be taken. How can the church act most redemptively? How can the church avoid years of fallout from the painful ordeal? Some might argue that there is little redemption in forced termination, but there are some situations where termination is seen as the only viable option. Still others would argue that the fallout is inevitable. Consenting both these possibilities, we feel there are steps which can be taken which would minimize the unbridled pain involved.

1. If all the steps have been taken to salvage the situation, then give the minister an opportunity to resign.

This step did not come easily. Please note the first phrase, "If all the steps have been taken to salvage the situation." When we first started this study of forced resignation, my personal prejudices were diametrically opposed. I felt that it would be best for the minister to require church action. In some situations, although remote, I still do believe that it would be best. However, upon close study of several rather sensitive situations, much of the pain could have been avoided if the minister had chosen to resign. This is true only if the situation is *hopelessly and ultimately terminal.*

How can the church and the minister determine if the situation is hopelessly and ultimately terminal? Although it appears to be hedging, I will admit that there is no clear way out. However, there are some indications. If the communications and negotiations have completely broken down, that is one sign.

If the alienations of the church and minister have become an embarrassment to the community, that, too, is a sign. If the church and minister have affected the positive witness for Christ in the community, then it can be safely judged that the alienations have become an embarrassment.

A pastor in Texas was asked by a "representative" group of persons to resign. They felt that the church's witness was being affected. They were embarrassed by the request, said the spokesman, but they felt it best for all. The minister did not agree. The acrimonious relationships began that Sunday afternoon. Members who had been faithful to the church for years stopped coming. Other members stopped speaking to the minister and his family. But the most demeaning events were the late-night phone calls. "Get out," one said, then hung up. "We are going to get you," said another and hung up. This went on for four months.

The minister said he knew that there were some who were going for the jugular when they poisoned his daughter's horse. Although most church members were above this kind of sadism, there were some in the church who were vicious enough to take these kinds of actions.

Unless there is overwhelming support for the minister under these circumstances, my personal opinion is that he should have resigned. He did not. A vote was taken. The majority, required by the church's constitution, voted in favor of asking the minister to resign. It will take years for the church to work through the grief. It may take even more

years for the church to work through the embarrassment
for those persons responsible for the reprehensible acts
committed.

But back to the minister. For the sake of the family, he
should have resigned. A family does not deserve this kind
of acrimony. The minister himself may feel strong enough
to contend with the conflict. His family must be considered
as well. Who can tell how much the daughter will have been
affected in her adult life? It is possible she may judge all
Christendom by the acts of a few.

Another sign is if the pulpit is being used for vindictiveness. If the minister begins an obvious vendetta, he should
be called to task. If a minister begins to name persons whom
he feels are responsible for the "disorder" in the church,
this is often an indication that the situation is hopelessly
and ultimately terminal.

There are other signs. In the vast majority of churches
that have been full of the people of God, enough wise persons will be able to isolate and decipher what other signs of
this situation are.

2. Be open about when and how the vote will be taken.

If the minister refuses to resign, and if the situation is
hopelessly and ultimately terminal, and, last, if the proper
steps according to the church's constitution and by-laws
have been taken, then announce openly to the church when
and how the vote will be taken. Give the church ample time
to consider the gravity of the situation. Communicate exactly what will be done.

A secret ballot is far preferable to a voice vote or a show
of hands. If some are embarrassed by their stand, it will
afford the luxury of "saving face" for years to come. In the
discussion of this statement about the preference of a secret
ballot, one young minister, who had just been forceably
terminated, replied, "That is the most cowardly act a

church could do. I do not agree that the vote should be taken by secret ballot."

There is some merit to the minister's view. If a church is a family, then the church should act like a family. A family fights. The fight is over, and they are still family. A family should have the right for each individual to express his or her views. When the fight or conflict has been resolved, then the family should still love the individual members.

In theory, the argument of a courageous open vote is valid. In point of fact, when there is enough conflict to force a minister to resign, the church has already reached divorce mentality. If a family loses a father by mutual consent of both the father and the mother and children, then the family is disturbed. The family unit is dead. A new family unit must be born if any part of the family is to survive. In the analogy, a church is a family unit disturbed. If an open vote is taken, the result could be eruptive. The church will need much more than a courageous open vote act to bring it back into the family unit.

3. Consider the feelings of the family of the minister.

Compassionate Christians care about people who hurt. Not only will the minister be hurt but the family as well. Avoid accusations and allegations about the family and encourage all church members to do the same.

The church will also want to consider the practical needs of the family. A spouse and children will be concerned about where they will live. If the church provides a parsonage, enough time should be given for the family to feel relatively secure in finding another place to live. Although time limitations will differ according to the needs of each situation, a minimum of *four to six months* should be allowed. This will give the minister an opportunity to search for another place to serve and find another place to live.

A minister and family who have been forced to resign

should be considered as servants of God. There is a ring of secular inhumanity in asking a family to vacate the premises in thirty days. A church is much more than a landlord. A minister and family are much more than tenants.

In my personal opinion, the four- to six-month allotment should be given even in extreme cases of immoral behavior of the minister. If the minister is guilty of immorality, the family should not have to suffer any more than absolutely necessary. Their feelings should be considered as the church decides the termination steps of the immoral minister. It is one thing to take punitive steps in termination toward the minister. It is quite another to take punitive steps in termination which affect the family of the minister.

4. Be fair in the severance financial package.

In the random sample of the persons who have been involved in forced resignations workshops during the past year, the severance financial package has ranged from zero to $14,000. Some churches appear to express their anger through some forms of financial punishment. (One pastor in Alabama shared that the treasurer, who was also the chairman of deacons, withheld the pastor's tithe in the last check given the pastor.) Other churches seem much more generous.

Almost half the persons who felt comfortable enough to share what the severance financial package was said they were given thirty days' salary. An equal amount of the persons were allowed to stay in the parsonage (when a parsonage was provided) for an additional thirty days after the salary was stopped.

Most ministers do not benefit from the unemployment funds provided by most businesses. The Employment Security Commission and the state Insurance Commission have not been cooperative in working out a possible unemployment program for ministers. The reasons are valid.

They feel the churches and the denomination need their own program.

To use Baptists as an example, The Southern Baptist Convention Annuity Board has no program for the unemployed minister. Those persons contacted do not at this time anticipate starting such a program.

The state Baptist convention in North Carolina has worked out a preliminary program for unemployed ministers. The proposal suggests a $100 initiation fee, and $50 per quarter, due the first day of the following months—first, fourth, seventh, and tenth of each year. The proposal began in 1984. Additionally, the proposal will include guidelines for churches dismissing a minister. The total family income of the Minister's Unemployment Fund in North Carolina will not exceed $700 per month. No one may receive assistance more than twice and a minimum of five years must elapse between the two.

Alabama, Tennessee, and Missouri Baptist conventions have rather defined ways of helping ministers who have been forced to terminate. The reality is that no convention can financially carry the minister and family for any length of time. Several state conventions have been able to "rescue," however.

Consequently, the burden of critical provisions rests on the churches where these ministers serve. Churches can develop some guidelines which will help them during these critical periods.

First, as stated earlier, the church should work hard at having a "grace" period of termination. That is, there should be some form of provision for the minister to find another church in which to serve. If this is impossible, the church should then consider compassionate alternatives to providing for the minister and family after termination. If the minister has found another church or if the minister has found another work, then the thirty days' termination pay is fair. If not, then the church should consider its moral responsibilities. A minimum of *four months' severance pay* should be allowed if the minister does not have a place to serve or a job.

Second, hospitalization, major medical, and life insurance programs should be continued for at least six months after termination. The two months' variance between severance pay is for the purpose of establishment. In most new work, the employee will need at least two months for the stabilization of insurance programs. This will alleviate the burden of having an "in-between" crisis where the minister has virtually no coverage.

Third, financial consultation should be afforded the minister if requested. In other words, many financial institutions will provide financial consultation at a minimal fee. The church could provide this financial consultation by an objective person outside the church if the minister requests.

The Career Guidance Section of the Church Administration Department, Baptist Sunday School Board, Nashville, Tennessee, provides this service for persons who have been in churches in the Southern Baptist Convention. Other denominations provide this kind of financial consultation. Most denominational institutions do not charge for this service. Financial institutions will charge only a minimal fee. Many ministers are not skilled at management of money. If caught in a vocational bind, many will be caught in a financial bind. The provision of this service will administer compassion in a practical way.

Fourth, credit cards and automobiles owned by the church should be returned immediately. No extension for the personal effects of the minister afforded by the church is necessary. These should be returned to a responsible person upon termination.

Fifth, what about moving expenses? If a minister has been terminated without a place to go, where will the moving expenses come from? Although this is above and beyond expectations (even of the minister himself or herself), moving expenses would be a generous gesture by a church who is trying desperately to heal the wounds of a difficult situation.

5. Should a church provide a reception for the minister and family?

Of the hundreds of ministers interviewed during the past several months, not one has had a positive experience with a reception provided by the church. Many of the ministers were provided receptions by individuals and groups of persons which they felt were a genuine expression of concern and love. On the other hand, when the church provided the reception, the result was a "washout."

The reasons seem apparent. The church has just voted to officially reject the minister. The church is now "celebrating" the occasion (at least, in the mind of the minister). Several spouses refuse to attend. In some cases, the ministers were given gifts ranging from financial gifts to television sets. But in each case discussed, the gift "felt" like a payoff. The minister will, in most cases, need the gift. In a church reception, it is demeaning to accept it.

Although each occasion is different, I would advise against it. The church may be trying to do what they feel is the mature thing to do. The minister, in attending, may feel it necessary to show class in being a "good loser." But the broad scope of the occasion merits little to celebrate. The memory of the occasion will hardly be positive. Indeed, it will more likely be negative. All things considered, it would be more merciful to omit the reception for the minister and the family.

If the church decides to provide a gift from the church, it would be better to have it given by a representative group of persons rather than at a reception.

6. Deal realistically with the "lame-duck" syndrome.

When the minister is terminated, he is in an awkward position. He has been called to minister. He has been contracted, although unofficially in most cases, to visit, witness to the lost in the community, lead worship, teach, administer the ordinances, and counsel the disturbed. He has a responsibility to do these and other activities. Now he is in an awkward position. He is ministering to the needs of some persons who are active participants in his leaving. He is leading worship for persons who no longer want him on the scene.

If a vote has been taken, the minister will be minimally effective after the vote. Give him or her a vacation for the remainder of the time negotiated. This is a merciful alternative in dealing with this painful period.

If the minister refuses a vacation (this is a frequent position, and often done in defiance), then make the best of a bad situation. Ask the minister for the privilege of staff or lay intervention in ministry. In other words, ask the minister for guidance in hospitalization visits for others in the church. Ask the minister for the privilege of lay intervention in the witnessing ministry of the church. The Bible Teaching program has a built-in program of outreach. Maximize this arm of the church during this time to relieve the minister of outreach responsibilities.

Personally, I feel it best to get another worship leader *immediately* if a vote has been taken to terminate the minister. I am a minister. I know how I would feel. It would be a difficult task to be objective for the next few weeks in leading the worship and preaching to the congregation. I am afraid I would disguise my anger under the umbrella of being prophetic. I would be tempted to use the Scriptures to discipline the sin in the church when in reality I would be venting the wrath of my grief. It is not easy to suffer rejection. It is almost impossible to disguise rejection.

No one expects a minister to lead the funeral services of his own wife. Although some ministers feel they must "hold up" after termination, most human beings feel this is a game being played to prove the minister is not human like the persons in the congregation. The congregation and the minister will be better off if another worship leader is selected immediately, avoiding the "lame-duck" syndrome.

7
After the Termination . . . The Minister

What are some redemptive steps for the minister after forced termination? It is easy to slip into a parental role and tell the son or daughter what they should do. It is more difficult to be brotherly to a colleague and share the pain. I want to do the latter.

1. Don't Drag the Body

You have been terminated. The divorce is final. Don't drag the body. Don't give in to the bittersweet taste of enjoying the pain. It is tempting to feel sorry for yourself and cling to the body. But for your purposes the body is dead. Walk away. As painful as the act will be, don't prolong the misery.

Help the church get worship leaders for the remainder of your time with the church. You are in no emotional state to lead worship. You will be helping yourself and the church by permitting someone else to lead the worship.

In many cases, you will be depending upon your spouse's work to provide income. Move to another part of town if this is true. Get as far away from the environment as your circumstances will allow.

2. Be Naive in Your Trust in God

Turn back the pages of history. Look back to the time your faith was naive. You know the complexity of faith. You know the disparaging character of mankind. You have been tempted to let your faith get more complex than life itself. Find again the simple trust in God that has gotten you through many difficult times before. Listen to God's Word again, my colleague, "Finally, be strong in the Lord, and in the strength of His might. Put on the full armor of God, that you may be able to stand firm against the schemes of the devil. Stand firm therefore, having girded your loins with truth, and having put on the breastplate of righteousness, and having shod your feet with the preparation of the gospel of peace" (Eph. 6:10-11,14-15).

The bottom line in this naiveté is to believe that God will provide you with your basic needs. He will not forsake you. He may not take care of you in the way you want Him to take care of you. But He will take care of you. He may not have your timetable. But He does have a timetable. He knows what He will do. Believe it.

3. Don't Disguise Your Sin

It is safe to say, there are no innocent parties. It is possible there has been injustice, perhaps even misjustice. But you should assume that a part of the fault lies in your own leadership and personal styles.

Your sin may be blatant. Some have been involved with others in immoral ways. Adultery, infidelity, and homosexuality are not complete strangers to ministers. If the sin of adultery, infidelity, or homosexuality is your sin, own it. The Scriptures have taught us ways to deal with sin. Confess your sin to God. Repent of your sin. That means to stop doing it. Turn your life around and recommit your purpose.

God does promise forgiveness, but He will not forgive if we do not repent.

Ministers who are conversant in theological jargon and biblical language are frequently insulted by this kind of straight talk. But the truth is that there is no other way to deal with it. If it is sin, then it should be treated as sin. You cannot rationalize your way out of sin simply because we know some of the psychological ramifications and causes. It should be treated in the same way that we advise others to treat it. Stop doing it. Ask God and other persons to forgive. Turn your directions back into focus again.

But confession and repentance will not keep your church. In most cases a blatant sin which is known by the church will cause churches to be put in an embarrassing position. Even though the church itself may forgive, the community probably will not. If the sin is blatant, a minister should not expect to be able to continue in his or her church.

The fact that you do not have a church does not mean you should court despair. There is hope. Start your life again. Some ministers have been able to take up their ministry again in another geographical location. If you have been called of God and know that church work is your purpose in life, you will certainly want to give it every opportunity. Many persons will help; those who will help will be discussed later.

Much attention has been given to those involved in blatant or obvious sin. The truth is that we were only able to find a few who were forced to terminate because of blatant or obvious sins. Most have been terminated because of other difficulties. But, if the sin is there, confess it and repent.

Too, we should not disguise sin that is not so obvious. Dishonesty, misuse of funds, greed, gluttony, vindictiveness, pride, arrogance, and sloth are but a few of the more clandestine sins of ministers. Whatever the sin, if we are in tune with the Holy Spirit of God and the convicting power of the Holy Spirit, we will know what we are guilty of. We should not disguise our sin.

4. Don't Fix Blame

The toughest decision a minister will make is whether or not to fix blame. It has been my experience that most ministers fix blame on themselves. These ministers speak angrily toward some of the persons they feel were responsible. But after some honest reflections, it is obvious that most of the blame is fixed on themselves. "What did I do wrong?" is a recurrent theme.

One minister told members of the personnel committee, "Draw up a list of the things you want me to do differently, and I will do them." There was something pathetic about that appeal. It assumes helplessness in repairing any damage from the minister's "own" initiative. If the personnel committee tells her what to do, then she will have no one to blame but herself. This feels like a no-win situation. The personnel committee will be reluctant to share what they feel are corrective measures. The minister, in this case a minister of education, will then feel a kind of universal blame on herself.

The personnel committee refused to draw up a "list." The minister of education resigned, having felt coerced. Then much energy was spent in blaming herself for the impossible situation. Perhaps it was inevitable. But, regardless, the minister of education is fighting a no-win situation by blaming herself for the impossible situation.

Don't fix blame on the visible spokesperson. Frequently, the persons who speak the most hurtful words are not the prime movers behind the forced termination. If the minister can remember this one fact, much mishandled hostility and fixing blame wrongly will be avoided.

Don't fix blame on the persons rumored to be responsible. Allies of the minister have been in the church much longer than the minister. These persons have had ample opportunity to develop relationships with several groups. Some of these relationships are not positive. Be careful to assess the situation carefully. Ask yourself, are the persons responsible really the persons who are rumored to be responsible? How much has gone on between the allies and other groups?

Most forced termination settings are complex. Usually, there are several sets of extenuating and circumventing circumstances. Do not be misled. The subplots that are going on are usually more dangerous than the plot itself. The "subterranean" pastors frequently are responsible for complex circumstances. It is a good idea to avoid fixing blame on any one person. In fact, although it may be virtually impossible because of our own humanity, it is a good idea to avoid blame altogether. That means avoiding taking the blame personally. It also means avoiding fixing blame on one or two persons or groups.

5. Take Preventive Maintenance Steps for Depression

As a minister, you have heard, "I just can't do anything about my depression." We did not believe it then. We must not believe it now that it is happening to us. We can do something about depression. By doing nothing, we are allowing depression to control our behavior. We must take some preventive maintenance steps to avoid having depression take control of our behavior.

Take a cold, calculating look at what you have going for you. How is your health? If it is good, rejoice. How is your outlook on your trainable skills? If you have taken stock of the things you can do, you know already that there is much to be grateful for. It is time to do something constructive about training those skills.

Work at being positive. There will be times that you are certain that you are playing games with yourself in trying to be positive. But if you work hard at being positive you will find it more and more credible.

Compare. There are some comparisons that may give very little optimism. But there are plenty of comparisons to give us our perspective back. No matter what the circumstances, there are some who have it more difficult. Compare your circumstances to those who have overcome even more horrendous obstacles. This process will give you hope and will help you deal with the potential depression.

Read again the Book of Job. Job is the story of a man who lost everything. He was rejected. He was betrayed. He was criticized by his "friends." No one believed him. In fact, Bildad, Eliphaz, Zophar, and Elihu, his religious friends, wanted to know what sins he had committed. Else, why would God forsake him? But as we remember, God had not forsaken him. God was giving Job the opportunity to work through the difficult times to establish his commitment to God.

Compare your setting with that of Job. This will help you to overcome depression. Remember also that Job had some tough times in combating his obstacles. He wanted to die. He prayed for God to kill him. He was depressed. But somehow he reached back for the strength that will help any believer in God work through depression.

6. Plan Your Vocational Direction for the Next Two Years

The most redemptive plan of survival is to plan specifically. Plan your time to fit the needs of what you want to become and what it will take to become what you want to become. Plan at least two years in advance. Five is even more preferable.

Write Out Your Vocational Objectives
Write out your plan and place it in a visible and conspicuous place. For example, one minister who was forced to

resign responded to this suggestion by writing, "I will refine my ministry skills and become more effective in my preaching, caring, and leading."

Write Out Your Specific Goals

Most ministers who have been forced to terminate want to get relocated quickly in another church. Some are too bitter. The latter often gravitate toward ambiguous vocational goals. But regardless of what kind of feelings or intentions, both should establish some specific goals about what they want to accomplish with their lives. An example of a specific goal to fit the vocational objective mentioned above would be, "By January 1, 19—, I will have attended one "J" term in seminary in the area of refining my interpersonal skills." (This is one month of training for graduate students and experienced ministers who want to continue their training.)

Still another practical goal for accomplishing a vocational objective would be, "By January 1, 19—, I will have developed a professional resumé for the purpose of distributing it to persons who might be helpful in relocation."

If a minister has decided upon a vocational redirection away from ministry, he will still need specific goals. For example, he may write, "By January 1, 19—, I will have completed a career assessment program to identify specific skills which can be refined for vocational redirection."

Write Out Specific Action Plans

After establishing and identifying vocational objectives, the specific goals will then be written. The next step in planning vocational directions for the next two years is to write out specific action plans for accomplishment.

Action plans are the result of asking How? When? How much? and Who will help me? For example, if the goal is "By January 1, 19—, I will have developed a professional

resumé for the purpose of distributing it to persons who
might be helpful in relocation," an action plan might be:

> *Consider professional consultation in developing a re-
> sumé by _____ (date).*
> *Isolate persons who will receive resumé by _____ (date).*
> *Identify persons who will be contacted by both personal
> interview and resumé by _____ (date).*
> *Considering postage, travel, payment to professional con-
> sultant, and miscellaneous expenses, the total cost of this
> action plan to accomplish the goal will be _____ (finan-
> cial amount).*

For every goal you have decided upon and written out,
you should now establish action plans to accomplish the
goal.

7. Take Financial Inventory

The crunch is on. The financial intake may be zero. It is
time to take a long, hard, calculating look at the financial
picture.

The surest way to take a financial inventory is to develop
a financial statement. You did this when you took out a
loan. Go to the bank and pick up a form that will help you
establish your financial statement. The banks we contacted
to consider the advisability of this option were willing to
give us the forms for the development of a financial statement. Your bank may charge a nominal fee, but most are
happy to give you the forms without charge.

A financial inventory will help you assess the value of
your real and personal property. Most of the ministers who
have been terminated have very little real or personal property. Almost all of them had "more" than they thought they
would have. Do not assume anything. Take a hard look at
what are assets and what are liabilities.

Consider bankruptcy as an absolute last resort. Too many extenuating circumstances surround the bankruptcy option. Property ownership is seriously limited. Loans will be difficult and in most cases impossible. There is a social stigma. There will be doubts about your ability to manage even the simplest of business negotiations. Avoid bankruptcy if possible.

Balance your intake and output. Be frugal. Almost all ministers find they can function, and in most cases function comfortably, with much less money than they have been using. You may find yourself, as have many, in the position of depending almost entirely for a few months on your spouse's salary. Allow for this possibility. Do not plan on more intake than you will have. It will be tempting to take out a personal loan to "tide you over," but remember you may be tiding over for longer than you planned. Be careful to anticipate only that which you know you can anticipate.

The first two necessities are food and shelter. Almost all large supermarkets have economy areas with generic and nonbrand foods. These are federally inspected foodstuffs on which you can save dollars. Shop with a balanced meal in mind. Know what you are going to the supermarket for and stick to it. The side trips in a supermarket are the cost items. The junk foods are expensive.

With shelter, decide what you absolutely must have to survive. You may need to store some furniture. Most economists agree that buying will be cheaper than renting. You may not have a choice. If you do not have the cost of a down payment, and you do not already own a home, renting may be your only option. Shop for good rental property. A house can be as inexpensive as an apartment.

The third necessity is not clothing. The third necessity is health insurance. Keep your medical insurance if at all possible. The health hazards of being without work are high. Your hospitalization and/or major medical insurance may end up being your most needed expenditure.

With loan repayment rates so high, you should think twice before trying to consolidate your bills. You may have more bills than you can pay. If you do, there are some practical steps to take. Write to each creditor and explain your situation. Most banks and large, reputable loan companies will afford you the luxury of paying only the interest (and not the premium) during your unemployment. They will not do this unless you ask. Face-to-face requests are appreciated. The face-to-face requests will be recorded and will be good credit-rating information when you get back on your feet.

Many insurance policies have cash value. Check your policy and see if you have this kind of equity. Most insurance policies have borrowing value. You can borrow on the cash value and not be penalized in some cases. In other words, you can use the money (your money) and pay it back without interest.

Avoid asking to borrow from friends. If they really care and have the resources, they may offer. In this case, use good judgment. Base your judgment on the past behavior of these friends. Nothing is quite so humiliating as having friends request repayment before you have offered to repay. You may lose something much more valuable than money— friends themselves.

Many antiques have marketable value. Recently, a colleague was about to purchase a new home. He needed cash for a down payment. He had inherited two antique harps but did not know their value, so he consulted an antique dealer. The dealer referred him to a catalog. My friend found similar items. He then consulted a "finder." (The "finder" was also referred by the antique dealer.) The "finder" found a purchaser for the antique harps, and the price was $32,000: a remarkable sum when you consider that the friend considered the possibility that they might not be marketable. A small percentage of the fee went to the "finder," and my friend had ample funds to supplement the down payment of his home. Look around. You may have something of marketable value. It will be worthless as an heirloom if you do not have the necessities to live.

Still another option for financial intake was suggested by Bruce Grubbs, a colleague who has done considerable research in the area of forced resignation. He suggests selling the home, investing the sum, and living off the interest. Consult a tax investor for the best process. Consider, as you do, the possibility that ministers will not get a double-dip tax break after 1985 on home ownership.

By all means, put yourself and your family on a budget. Keep to the budget. Allow for bare necessities. Write down what you have spent. Compare the unplanned expenditures weekly. By writing these down and reminding yourself and your family, you will see what you are spending much more clearly.

8. Consider All Available Denominational Resources

For the Southern Baptist pastor, a state convention may help. An example is North Carolina. Guided by the chairmanship of Burrel Lucas of the Baptist state convention in North Carolina, a Minister Care Team proposal was presented to the North Carolina Baptist Convention in October 1983 in Cary, North Carolina. Under the umbrella of a Minister's Unemployment Fund, ministers whose family income does not exceed $700 per month will be provided with help. This is available for those churches and ministers who participate in a fund developed by $100 initiation fee, and $50 per quarter by the church.

Other state conventions which provide some assistance are Tennessee, South Carolina, Virginia, Alabama, Georgia, Louisiana, Mississippi, Florida, Kentucky, Missouri, Texas, and Arkansas. Although other state Baptist conventions may offer help, these states have adopted policies of assistance with which we are familiar. In most cases the assistance is supplied through the auspices of the executive secretary or executive director and the church-minister-relations director of these states.

Some associations provide emergency funds and assistance for ministers and their families. Also, some churches have provided emergency assistance. For confidential treatment, consult your church-minister-relations director in the state convention. Additional help and guidance will be given, upon request, from the Church Administration Department, through the Career Guidance Section.

Contrary to what many think, personal contact with the church-minister-relations directors and the Career Guidance Section will help, not hinder, your future plans. You will find us a group of brothers who share your pain. We will do our best to find redemptive solutions to a thorny problem. We have taken seriously Resolution 9, adopted by the Southern Baptist Convention in Pittsburgh, Pennsylvania in June 1983, which encouraged our further exploration and guidance for ministers who have been forced to terminate their ministry in their churches.

9. Consider All Available Federal Assistance Programs

You have paid your taxes. If you are forced to opt for food stamps you should know how to get them. Local, state, and federal assistance programs will vary. Find the specific offices where you will go to get help if you are forced to do so. The county courthouse, the Federal Building, and the state Unemployment Commission will guide you in finding the appropriate channels. The process is long and tedious. It may be humiliating. But you should know where to go, and you should know under what circumstances you are entitled to assistance.

10. Learn to Tolerate Ambiguity

One parting suggestion for the minister who has been terminated—learn to tolerate ambiguity. Certainty will be a luxury. The future will be unpredictable. You may have some friends like Eliphaz, Bildad, Zophar, and Elihu. These friends may be asking with pharisaical cynicism what you have done wrong. These friends did not understand Job's situation. Your friends will be hard pressed to understand your situation. The best skill you may learn is the ability to tolerate ambiguity. There will be no certainty for some time.

The need for certainty is a trap. Like the prophets of the Old Testament, you will want a sign from God that He still loves you. You may be tempted to ask God to prove Himself again since it appears He has forsaken you. But remember that the Pharisees did the same. "And the Pharisees came out and began to argue with Him, seeking from Him a sign from heaven, to test Him. And sighing deeply in His spirit, He said, 'Why does this generation seek for a sign? Truly I say to you, no sign shall be given to this generation' " (Mark 8:11-12).

In other words, God does not have to prove that He exists. He does not need to prove to you that He has not forsaken you. Certainty is not the proof that God exists. Faith is the certainty that God exists. Your faith will prove that God has not forsaken you. Faith affords the luxury that you can live with ambiguity.

11. Accepting an In-Between Job Is Not Defeat

You may be forced to become a temporary tentmaker. This does not signify defeat. This only means you have planned to fill the interim with meaning. You will want to consider all the options for wage earning if you fall on desperate times. An hourly wage-earning job can be fulfilling and not stressful if you permit it to be so. The fact is that in some states you will be fortunate to get an hourly wage-earning job.

12. Do Not Lose Your Dream

A friend of mine loved to quote a little homily, "Suffering will make you bitter or it will make you better." If you lose your dream, it will make you bitter. If you maintain your dream, it will make you better. Your dream will be more visible and more in focus.

Remember, Paul was stoned, imprisoned, cursed, ridiculed, and forsaken. Jesus was tortured, jailed, and crucified. To be without work seems comparatively small. It is not small. But compared with what it costs for some, it is. Work at maintaining your dream in the face of adversity.

13. Remember Your Family

It is tempting to get so caught up in our own hurts that we forget that our family is suffering with us. They are empathetic. They hurt with us. They are suffering the same dehumanizing feelings that we are facing.

Stop long enough to remember that you have the love of your family. Like you, they have been rejected by people who should have loved them. Like you, they are numb from the shock. This is a time to reach out for each other. This is a time to find strength in the family love that has helped you to weather all kinds of storms in the past. And finally, this is the time that can draw you back to the real focus of God's first institution, the family.

14. Don't Give Up

One minister told me, "Brooks, I have thrown in the towel." When I suggested to him that I understood his feelings but not his plan, he laughed. "Well," he said, "It's obvious you have never been there!" But I have. I have been to the point of wanting to throw in the towel. Something keeps me from doing it.

There must be something to reach back for. Call it grit! Call it determination! Call it tenacity! Something will keep you from giving up if your commission from God is defined. You will come to a time when the only thing left is your call. It must be defined. It must be clear. But don't give up.

15. Join a Support Group

Find other ministers who have been forced to resign. Meet regularly with them. Find strength from each other. Your church minister relations director or a similar person in your denomination will help you find such a group. The Career Guidance Section, Baptist Sunday School Board, 127 Ninth Avenue, North, Nashville, Tennessee 37234, will help you start such a group.

If you find you need professional help to get you through a difficult time in your life, you can receive assistance, both financial and referral, through the Career Guidance Section. Contact Dr. Brooks Faulkner at the Career Guidance Section address or your state church minister relations director (or the equivalent in your denomination).

8
After the Termination . . . The Church

What are some redemptive steps for the church after forced termination of the minister? The deed has been done. There are those who are guilty. There are those who are innocent. There are those who have known the inside story from the beginning. There are those who have not had the slightest idea of what was going on in the church during the incident. What must the church do? Where can the church turn? This chapter is a suggested agenda for the church after the minister has been terminated.

1. Share, Don't Hide, the Information

One of the basic tenets of many denominations is the priesthood of every believer. What this means to us as individuals is that we are all responsible. No one can be guiltless. On the other hand, no one is totally responsible. The priesthood of every believer gives us the right to have information.

"There are some things that are better left unsaid," the chairman of deacons said upon questioning from a church member.

"But why did we ask him to resign?" the member insisted.

"It is better that just the deacons have that information," the chairman replied.

"But what possible good can that do? Don't you know that if people do not have information, they will create their own facts?"

Although the conversation may be apocryphal, the attitude is real for many. Some persons feel that the reasons for forcing resignation are privileged information. This is true in the bureaucratic structure of most businesses. It is not true for the church. "But if he does not listen to you, take one or two more with you, so that by the mouth of two or three witnesses *every fact may be confirmed.* And if he refuses to listen to them, *tell it to the church*" (Matt. 18:16-17a, author's italics).

Every church member has the right to know information that is pertinent to a decision for which all are responsible. Deacons are not justified, biblically, in keeping information from church members. Deacons are not to represent the best decision-making processes of church members. That violates the basic belief of the priesthood of the believer.

Information about forced resignations of ministers is not pleasant. But church members have a right to that information.

Unshared information will leave a great deal to the imagination. Without accurate information, there will be "good guys" and "bad guys" (no sex discrimination intended) and often the "bad guys" are those who feel the information is too sensitive to share with the hoi polloi. Withholding information is insulting. It is demeaning. It will help very little in solving the problem of grief.

On a more positive note, shared information helps everyone share in the responsibility of the decision. The decision is rarely clear when a minister is forced to resign. There are almost always complex circumstances. But with all the information the entire church body will make a responsible decision. To believe in this process is to confirm one of the most precious beliefs of the church.

How should the information be shared? That is a difficult question. It is my prejudiced opinion that it is rarely best shared publicly. It would be better to have groups of persons share in smaller groups the entire circumstances around the incident. Rather than making an announcement with intimate details in the worship service, an informal discussion in a business meeting would be preferable. Even if the vote will be or has been taken during a Sunday service, the discussion would be more appropriate in smaller groups.

One church in Missouri followed a rather unique process. After the vote was taken on Sunday morning after the worship service, an announcement was made that on Sunday afternoon, several deacons would be at the church in Sunday School rooms to discuss the entire episode. Five rooms were designated. Three deacons were assigned to each room. Church members picked the deacons with whom they were most comfortable and went to that room. The deacons stayed from 2:00-4:00 PM. The church member sharing this process felt they answered most of the volatile questions with candor and tenderness. She felt that the church dealt with a difficult problem in a redemptive way.

2. Be Fair in Severance Pay

Some will be tempted to punish the minister financially. One church member wrote, "We do not owe him anything. He betrayed us. He deserves to be without work." With the kind of anger that frequently accompanies a forced resignation, this person's feelings are certainly understandable. Many will feel the way this person did. But this is a time for cooler heads and more compassionate hearts.

As suggested earlier, thirty days' pay is not enough. Four to six months' severance pay is fair. Your church should remember that there is a stigma to being forced to resign from a church. Other churches do not welcome the minister forced to resign. Churches are reluctant to even consider such a person. One church member wrote, "Our church assumes that if a minister has been forced to resign, then there must be something wrong with him." That position is widespread. When your church asks the minister to resign, the feelings of other churches about ministers who have been asked to resign should be considered in the severance pay.

The family should be considered. The leadership effectiveness of the minister may have been null and void. The minister's spouse is rarely to blame. The children cannot answer for the minister. The entire family will be searching for another place to live and food to eat; other ongoing needs are to be cared for.

The school system should be considered. A minister with children must arrange for changing schools. In most cases this is one of the more complex issues surrounding the problem. Give the minister time to work this problem out. An adequate severance package will relieve one of the pressures of trying to find a school system that will fit the entire needs of the family.

Medical insurance should also be considered. One compassionate church in Texas arranged for the families' medical insurance (hospitalization and major medical) to be taken care of for one year following the forced resignation. We recommend that at least a six-month provision be made by churches. This will afford the minister time to get settled in a new position and arrange for establishment of medical insurance.

One very important reason for this six-month provision is the length of time it takes to establish medical insurance. If there are medical problems with any member of the family, most insurance companies will be reluctant to establish a policy immediately.

Marketability of the minister should be considered in severance pay. Several inquiries and research projects have been conducted on the age most churches prefer when considering a minister. Although extenuating circumstances affect each decision, most churches prefer a minister between the ages of thirty-five and forty-five years of age. This is not true for youth ministers and ministers of music. (These ages are younger.) It is true for other ministers, including pastor, minister of education, associate minister, church business administrator, and pastoral care leader.

If the minister who has been forced to resign is fifty-four years of age, it is reasonable to expect the church to treat him with more consideration, simply because of his age, in severance packages. The chances of relocation of a fifty-four-year-old minister are not usually as good as if he were forty.

Because the issue of forced resignation is unpleasant, unpleasant stories surface. One such story about a severance package happened in a church in Alabama. The treasurer, who was also chairman of deacons, was one of the principal spokespersons in asking the minister to resign. Conflict had frequented the relationship between the pastor and him. When the vote was taken, no mention was made of the severance package. The treasurer took it upon himself to make the decisions.

The custom was that the minister pick up his check in person on Monday morning from the treasurer. This, in itself, was demeaning. Symbolically, the treasurer was in charge of the payment.

So on Monday morning following the vote on Sunday, the minister went by the deacon's home to pick up his check. The minister was given a check for two weeks in advance. "I have taken out your tithe from the payment since we would like to have you out by the end of the week. We will get someone else to lead the worship service next Sunday. That will mean you will not be here next Sunday. Since you will not be here, I went ahead and took out your tithe, since

you know we need it." The minister said he was so stunned
he didn't argue.

Very few situations will be this unpleasant. The church
will want to be compassionate in the severance package. I
doubt if you will want to take out the tithe before the minister has an opportunity to give.

3. Consider Shifting the Leadership Load

This step following termination of the minister is much
more delicate. You will want to consider the wisdom of
shifting the leadership load. Those persons who have been
visible in lay leadership during the minister's difficult last
days will have created some negative feelings for those in
the membership who were sympathetic to the minister. The
minister is now terminated. The lay leadership should be
considered for possible adjustment. For example, a chairman of deacons who has been the spokesperson for the deacons and the persons who were unhappy with the minister
will want to consider the wisdom of stepping into a less
visible role. This will allow healing. As long as the person
who symbolizes the antagonists is still visible, the volatile
situation will continue.

Obviously, this is not a hard and fast rule. There are
exceptions. A church should use wisdom in deciding if the
shift is advisable. Ask, will a shift in lay leadership visibility
increase or diminish healing?

4. Consider Calling an Interim Pastor

A wise and spiritually stable person for interim pastor
can provide rich and lasting dividends. The church has just
gone through a divorce. It would be foolish to jump into a
new marriage with a new minister. Time alone will not
heal. But the wisdom and strength of a person serving as
interim, coupled with time, will heal.

What kind of person should a church consider? If the

troubled waters are still rippling, some characteristics of the interim should be conspicuous. This person should have had the experience of dealing with conflict effectively. This person should have the skill of preaching redemptively as well as evangelistically. He should have the ability to bring the church back to the focus of its mission. What are they about? Where are they going? Do they still believe they are the people of God? These are some of the questions this person should be able to help the church deal with.

Where should the church look to find a wise and stable interim pastor? In the Baptist denomination, the directors of missions in each association will lend able and sound advice about where to find an interim pastor. Usually these persons are not able to become interim pastors themselves, but they have access to those persons who are able. State denominational leaders can lend helpful advice. The church-minister-relations directors in the states have communication lines with persons who specialize in dealing with the healing period after forced termination. Retired ministers who have been through the battles of normal church conflicts often have the resources to help churches for brief periods of time to work through difficult situations.

Avoid calling as interim pastor a person who is a potential candidate as pastor. This will avoid the possible hidden agendas which can hinder progress in healing. A potential pastor who is serving as interim pastor can hardly be expected to be objective about the contributions of a previous minister who was forced to resign. It will be essential for the church to see the positive contributions of the former minister if they are to weigh the problem with clarity and honesty. A potential pastor will have more temptation to build off the negative factors of the former minister than would an interim minister.

An interim pastor can help the church decide what kind of leader they want and expect. The process for finding the right person for each church is easily aborted. The persuasive power of spiritual jargon can mislead a church. A church member who is a responsible leader should be careful when using the words, "This is God's chosen person for our church." He or she may feel that deeply. But church members are impressionable. When "God's choice" or "God's will" is used, the phrase is powerfully seductive. Persons do not wish to go against "God's choice" or "God's will." Church members should be afforded the luxury of deciding if they, too, feel a person is "God's choice." Overzealous church members can get excited with their vocabulary and get a church in deep commitment to a person before the church really wants to be committed.

An interim pastor can help the church avoid spiritual jargon that might lead to spiritual jeopardy. An interim pastor can help the church ask the right questions about what kind of leader the church wants and needs. Is the primary thrust of the congregation evangelistic? Is reaching persons for Christ the major interest of the church? If so, then a person who is strong in evangelism should be considered. Even then, the interim minister can help the church decide if they want a person who is strong in evangelistic preaching or evangelistic witnessing. Does the church want a leader who is strong in helping people work together? If so, then the interim minister can help the church to find this kind of person.

Although every church will want a minister who is strong in evangelism, witnessing, pastoral care, administration, and interpersonal relations, the church should recognize that these persons are very rare indeed. Some strengths and skills will outweigh others. An interim can help the church know better what is needed at this particular juncture in history.

5. Anticipate Losing Some Members

You may not, but the church can expect to lose some members. During a minister's tenure, it is normal for a minister to develop close and intimate friends. These friends may be loyal and dedicated to the position of the minister. It is predictable that these persons are going to have a difficult time in adjusting to the church without the minister. If the possibility for losing some members is allowed in the thinking of the leaders of the church, it will lessen the pain. Losing some members may cause the church to suffer needless guilt unless the possibility of losing them is anticipated.

6. Select Mature Members of the Minister Selection Committee

No one step can bring the church back to normalcy. But if any one step could, it would be in the selection of mature members of the minister selection committee. Find the persons who are representative of the church. Find those persons who will not overreact to the pain the church has grown through. These persons should be able to converse intelligently about the hopes and dreams of the church. Also, they should be able to deal with the problem of forced termination with candor and honesty. Avoid involving those persons who were too emotionally involved in the previous problem.

7. Trust the Process

Trust is difficult. Under any circumstances, trust is built slowly. But after forced termination, trust is especially difficult. Your church may feel they have been "burned." When church members are bothered with the feeling of having been "burned," they become cautious. Many become suspicious. Suspicious persons cannot trust.

The democratic process is imperfect, but it is the best process of church government. Trust God and trust His people. The democratic process will give you hope. Time will not heal. But believing that the best interests of God's people will be served through trusting the process will heal.

8. Reestablish Respect for Ministers

The minister has lost respect. The church needs to work on the area of reestablishing respect for the minister. Formally, biblical studies should be conducted on the office and work of the minister. Informally, leaders should isolate the constructive contributions ministers have made in the churches.

Conclusion

I considered all kinds of cheap advice when I started this project. I thought of recommending to churches that they be certain that they have a mature minister who is the right person before calling a minister. But then how can anyone be certain? We do the best we can in deciding what is God's will for a church. We have no adequate measurements for emotional and spiritual maturity of ministers. You find the process that works best and implement that process. You hope you have found the right person. So, to be certain is cheap advice.

I considered recommending to ministers that they check out the history of the church in the area of forced termination. Does the church have a history of frequent forced termination of ministers? I still think that is a good idea. But there are so many ambiguous areas that I am not certain that should be the deciding criterion for deciding against a church. So suggesting that a minister study the church's history of forced termination is cheap advice.

I don't think we need to revert back to the unquestioning regard for ministers that was apparent in our early history in the United States. The fear of ministers may have done more damage than we know. It may be that our latent anger as a nation toward the spiritual mystique of ministers of yesteryear is a major cause of forced termination. We no longer need the attitude from ministers, "When you question me, you question God." We are wiser now. We know he or she is human. Humanity causes weakness and vulnerability. These persons are no longer the angelic untouchables.

We do need to seek God's guidance. We need to pray earnestly and seriously about the decisions to call a minister. Ministers need to pray earnestly and seriously about accepting the call from a church. Ministers need to pray that they are not swept up in the inebriation of going to a "better situation." Larger churches, larger budgets, bigger buildings, and urban settings do not necessarily mean "better situations."

We need to work on finding a "fit." A church's personality should "fit" the leadership strengths of the minister. God designed our creative potential. He expects us to maximize that potential. God allows for the distinctive personality of a church. He expects both ministers and church to work to "fit" the blending of the two.

We must avoid the "rescue" mentality of ministers. In an effort to be rescued, many ministers move to another church. Most find many of the same problems they have left. As in a lasting marriage, a minister needs to get prepared for the marriage to the church. To follow the analogy, he should leave from the right dock and prepare for a long voyage. He should not put out to sea and wait to be rescued.